Teamwork

A Guide to Successful
Collaboration in
Health & Social Care

Sue Hutchings
Judy Hall
Barbara Lovelady

Speechmark Publishing Ltd
Telford Road, Bicester, Oxon OX26 4LQ, UK

Published by

Speechmark Publishing Ltd, Telford Road, Bicester, Oxon OX26 4LQ, UK
www.speechmark.net

First published 2003

002-4761/Printed in the United Kingdom/1010

British Library Cataloguing in Publication Data
Hutchings, Sue
    Teamwork : a guide to successful collaboration in health and social care
    1. Health care teams   2. Social service – Teamwork
    3. Interpersonal relations
    I. Title   II. Hall, Judy   III. Lovelady, Barbara
    362.1'068

ISBN 0 86388 276 5

Dedication

For the students and staff at the School of Health and Social Care,
Oxford Brookes University.

About the Authors

Sue Hutchings is a lecturer in Occupational Therapy at the School of Health Care, Oxford Brookes University. Her clinical background as an Occupational Therapist is in psychiatry, particularly in community mental health. In her role as an educator, she has been involved in designing and delivering pre-registration multi-professional education for undergraduate health and social care professionals.

Judy Hall is a senior quality assurance co-ordinator for education and training for the Department of Health. She was previously Head of the Rehabilitation Studies Department at the School of Health Care, Oxford Brookes University. Her clinical background is as a physiotherapist working in a general hospital before setting up a community physiotherapy service. Her teaching interests include human anatomy, biomechanics and health care of the older person.

Barbara Lovelady is a lecturer practitioner at the School of Health Care, Oxford Brookes University. Her clinical background is in cardiac and critical-care nursing, both in Australia and the United Kingdom. She enjoys teaching on a variety of multi-professional courses, both in practice and University settings. Currently, her primary educational responsibility is the management and development of intensive and high-dependency care programmes.

Contents

CONTENTS

Tables

Figures

Foreword

THE ISSUE OF COLLABORATION between the helping professions has been on the agenda for a very long time, and the present government is placing strong and increasing emphasis on working together, with the patient or client at the very centre of the caring and curing process.

However, the fact that it still seems to be necessary to underline the importance of joint working shows that it has not been easy to achieve it in practice. There have been lots of pilot schemes over the years, and there are today many examples of good collaborative practice, but putting the client first has proved to be a very hard thing to do on a consistent and continuing basis. Professional boundaries have sometimes been a barrier to progress, and sometimes professionals have feared 'losing ground' to other professional groups.

It is easy to say that preparation for collaboration ought to start at the beginning of people's professional studies, but knowing how to do that is not obvious. This book is rooted in a practical understanding of what it means to collaborate, and of how to help students learn to do it and keep on doing it until collaboration is just an integral part of practice. I am sure that teachers of students on both pre-registration and continuing professional development programmes will find it invaluable, and so too will current practitioners wishing to refresh their understanding of working together.

This is a book with its 'feet' on the ground, but which is also on top of the more theoretical perspectives that need to inform and illuminate practice. The authors have lived collaboration in the creation of an innovative, multi-professional programme at Oxford Brookes University, so they know what they are talking about. It is a timely volume, and one that will stand new, and not so new, practitioners in good stead as we all seek to make joined-up care an everyday reality.

Professor Linda Challis
Deputy Vice Chancellor (Academic Affairs)
Oxford Brookes University

Preface

PREFACE

WELCOME TO *Teamwork: A Guide to Successful Collaboration in Health and Social Care.* The purpose of this book is to act principally as a guide to key concepts, ideas, policies and politics that are involved in multi-professional teamworking today. It will focus on the notions that we are all still in the process of learning about the craft of working together, and that there are no absolutes, definitive protocols, or a point where we can stop and say, 'Yes, I know it all now!'

We have started our exploration of multi-professional teamworking with the implicit assumption that the most important outcome to this way of working is better quality care for clients, and more person-centred, needs-led health and social care services. We accept that many practitioners and many services may already fully embrace the values and practice of collaboration. However, we also acknowledge that in today's world, health and social care policies and theories can evolve and be disseminated at an ever-increasing speed, making the simple act of keeping up-to-date and informed difficult and exhausting.

We hope this book will act as a series of 'signposts' to help make some sense of the concepts, ideas and theories underpinning collaborative working, and to help illuminate the implications this has for practice and professional development. It is not intended as a definitive source of evidence that collaboration works, but rather as a practically orientated 'helicopter view', based on our own thoughts, research and experiences.

Successful collaboration seems to be a blend of particular ingredients and, on paper, it sounds so straightforward and matter of fact. However, the realities are that it can be hard work and demanding, built on a multi-professional team understanding, and valuing key professional and personal differences, as well as establishing commonalties. As a guide, we hope that this book will develop your understanding of the nature of collaboration, and provide you with some ideas on how to begin or nurture collaboration in your own workplace setting. It may take two to tango, but it takes a co-ordinated team to stage the ball!

Finally, we hope this book will help today's practitioners feel that they have a lot of skills to contribute and, through positive collaboration, can enhance the quality of care and therapy for clients and carers.

Acknowledgements

We wish to thank Janice Childs, Jayne Comins, Sally Davis, Kevin Reel and Trish Westran for all their help with the writing of this book – particularly their contributions to 'In their Own Words'.

Introduction
Using this Book as a Guide to Collaborative Working

Sections

This book is organised into five sections, which address different aspects of collaborative working. Within each section are a number of chapters, which explore the section's theme from a variety of perspectives.

The book starts with three reflective accounts of 'learning by doing' (Section A), in order to highlight the issues, concepts and skills explored in subsequent sections. Section B (Understanding the Nature of Collaboration) focuses principally on understanding the background context of collaborative working. Section C (The Benefits of Collaboration) discusses the advantages and positive benefits of collaborative working. Section D (Preventing Collaboration) goes on to consider the barriers and drawbacks to collaborative working. Section E (Demonstrating Collaboration) provides detailed descriptions of the skills required for collaborative working.

Note that the Appendix contains an integrated case study that draws together the skills, knowledge and attitudes that underpin multi-professional collaboration, as discussed in Section E.

Chapters

Progressing through each section, the chapters conclude with a summary of key points.

In Sections C and E, chapters conclude with an opportunity to formulate an action plan for personal and/or service development. These chapters are further supplemented by opportunities to reflect, either on an individual basis, or in small groups 'thinking time' to consolidate understanding and prompt further discussion.

Where appropriate, illustrative examples or case vignettes provided by practitioners have been used to highlight key points ('In their own words').

Terminology

For the purposes of clarity and consistency, the term 'client' is used to denote people who use a health- or social care service (as in client, service user, consumer). In particular cases where a specific health or social care context is discussed, the most appropriate term is used.

'Multi-professional collaboration' is used as the preferred term to describe multi-disciplinary teamwork across a range of client groups and health and social care settings. The different terms used to describe this way of working are highlighted in Section B, Chapter 5.

'Health and social care professional' is used as the preferred term to indicate the range of practitioners and workers involved in planning and delivering health and social care. The principles of collaborative working are equally applicable to support workers and assistants, and people employed in the voluntary and private sectors.

'Client-centred care' is used as a generic term to encompass a broad spectrum of health and social care interventions – from direct care as an in-patient in hospital, to more community-based rehabilitation and associated support services. Implicit in this term, regardless of setting, is the notion of the individual client's needs and wishes being central to the planning and delivery of health and social care.

Completing an action plan

This book offers you an opportunity to devise some personal and/or professional goals to develop your understanding and implementation of collaborative working.

It is important that goal-setting is realistic and attainable if it is going to be a constructive prompt for action. The established SMART criteria can be a useful framework for setting goals:

S – Specific (has a detailed focus)
M – Measurable (change can be observed/recorded in some way)
A – Achievable (it is possible to do within realistic parameters)
R – Relevant (it is a goal actually worth pursuing)
T – Timely (a timescale or deadline for completion can be identified).

SECTION A

LEARNING BY DOING: PERSONAL REFLECTIONS ON COLLABORATION

CHAPTER 1

An Occupational Therapist's Account

MY OWN EXPERIENCES AS A PRACTITIONER have very much influenced how I approach and engage with multi-professional collaboration. Early on in my occupational therapy career, I worked in community mental health and with a small multi-professional team. I was fortunate enough to be part of a newly evolving service, and those experiences have shaped my attitudes, and developed particular skills and personal attributes.

As part of this new initiative, I worked in a number of geographical community-based locations, and with a range of professionals in primary healthcare, from institutional settings and the voluntary sector, as well as with social services personnel. The service functioned as a core team of an occupational therapist and community psychiatric nurses (CPNs), being supplemented at specific community bases by peripheral team members such as psychologists, social workers, general practitioners and psychiatrists.

Although community mental health services have moved on considerably and now provide more integrated community services in terms of assertive outreach and the Care Programme Approach (CPA), the spirit of shared endeavour remains a potent memory. However, looking back now it is interesting to note how much my own profession has developed its unique body of knowledge into a more coherent whole. Perhaps this is true for all the professions, as with an ever-changing context for health- and social care, professions often have to 'reinvent' themselves and reaffirm their particular skills or knowledge.

In this respect, my one regret is not being able to articulate clearly or confidently enough what my own profession-specific role was to the multi-professional team. At the time, I thought I was clear about the contribution occupational therapy could make within a community mental health context. However, this was often difficult when practising in a non-traditional setting and without a profession-specific role model to emulate, or any guiding theories that translated into a community context.

I can remember getting quite immersed and excited by the very evident support that collaborative working brings, and enjoying the opportunity to pool ideas and share goal-setting and problem-solving. A certain amount of role-blurring and overlap can be a healthy process in collaboration, but I feel effective collaboration benefits from team members being clear about their unique skills and confident about their professional identity. Naturally, this process of professional socialisation matures with time and experience, but unless practitioners start their careers with a kernel of profession-specific absolutes, then it can mean that any prospect of future collaboration is a muddle of weaknesses and uncertainties as opposed to a synergy of strengths.

My most recent experience of collaboration has been in the educational context, specifically with undergraduate pre-registration students from across a range of disciplines (all nursing pathways, midwifery, physiotherapy and occupational therapy). I have witnessed the development of a newly formed school of healthcare, and have been part of the process of planning and delivering a multi-professional curriculum. This has entailed working with colleagues and students across different disciplines, which has had an undeniable impact on my own professional identity and what it means to be an occupational therapy educator.

I have noted that it does take time as well as the opportunity to develop constructive ways of working. Initially, there is that sense of being unsure and having to navigate through a complexity of unfamiliar concepts and terminology. It could be easier simply not to bother, or to pay lip service to the notion of 'collaboration', while continuing to mutter darkly in corners about 'the nurses' or 'the occupational therapists', and doing the polite minimum. However, over time (and this doesn't have to be years) it can be possible to get to a real sense of the whole being greater than the sum of its parts, and that a qualitative difference is evident in the way a collaborative team thinks and acts.

The hub of the question is whether collaboration and learning to collaborate is a useful skill for students to acquire. This can be debated from a range of perspectives, including the view that learning to collaborate is best left to post-graduate and post-qualifying education, as then students have an immediate and relevant practice context. My own view is that students need to learn how to collaborate – not necessarily practice collaborative working in a particular context *per se,* but need to be sensitised and prepared for the world of work. By being prepared and open to the benefits of collaborative working, they are more likely to engage in innovative service developments and be more circumspect about taking risks in terms of developing ideas without feeling personally or professionally threatened. It is now the remit of education to devise the most effective way of helping students to develop those skills of collaboration. Such a curriculum and its learning methods need to be relevant to the students' experience and stage of professional development, and need to rise above the practical and logistical problems that can so often overwhelm complex, multi-professional educational initiatives.

If I had a 'tip' to pass on, it would be to say that in order to work collaboratively, you often discover how alike, but also how different professional groups are. I think it is necessary to view collaboration along a continuum of differences and similarities. Multi-professional collaboration cannot be neatly parcelled into being exclusively about differences; nor is it always a mutual meeting of minds. In terms of teaching, having generic examples of key healthcare principles is useful, as it places health- and social care in a broader and more relevant socio-political context. However, being able to talk in an informed way about your own practice and professional perspective is equally important, as this can be useful exposure to how different professionals think and act.

I think that the common misconception about multi-professional working is that if we all knew, exactly, what each other actually does then everything will be hunky-dory. Although this can be helpful in a specific practice context, in the abstract it is rarely meaningful. It can provide a 'snapshot' or a soundbite of what a particular professional does, but this may not endure or represent the scope of practice and the extent of variation within a professional group. In a sense, it does come down to learning and continuing to learn, and it is that dynamic that means we all need to revise, review, update and rethink. This may mean we encounter a few surprises or setbacks on the way, but it can also mean that we learn from and about each other in a positive way that enhances the quality of professional practice and ensures a better service to our clients.

Thinking time: learning by doing

1 What, for you, are the key points about multi-professional collaboration, highlighted by this account?

a _____

b _____

c _____

2 How is this person's account similar to, or different from your own experiences?

3 Does this account raise any advantages or disadvantages of multi-professional collaboration?

- For the client?

- For the service?

- For the employer?

- For the health- and social care professions?

Forward planning: using this book as a series of 'signposts'

Consider how subsequent sections in this book may help you to gain a fuller picture of the issues raised in this account.

So, what is multi-professional collaboration?
Section B Understanding the Nature of Collaboration
See Chapters 4, 5 and 6.

But what is there to be gained from working collaboratively?
Section C The Benefits of Collaboration
See Chapters 7, 8, 9 and 10.

But how feasible is multi-professional collaboration?
Section D Preventing Collaboration
See Chapters 11, 12 and 13.

What do you actually have to do to work collaboratively?
Section E Demonstrating Collaboration
See Chapters 14, 15, 16, 17 and 18.

CHAPTER 2

A Nurse's Account

THIS IS A PERSONAL VIEW OF COLLABORATION and how my own experiences have brought me to this point in my career. I remember as a student being so anxious to learn how to be an effective nurse that I don't recall ever learning much about other healthcare professionals, except for nurses in different specialist areas. Maybe we did, but it was a low priority and 'not essential to know' in order to get through the challenging task of completing a course and doing clinical hours. We were paid in the workforce when I trained as a nurse, and there was no grant to pay off. I recognise that today there is even more pressure on student nurses, and I wonder if learning about multi-professional teamwork ranks as high on the priority list as qualifying as a professional nurse?

As my professional career developed, and my role was increasingly that of liaison with other members of the team, I became acutely aware of the importance of multi-professional collaboration. I observed incidents in practice where the communication chain broke down completely, resulting in cancelled patient discharges, and conflicting information being given to patients about their illness, especially at a time when consistency was crucial. I also witnessed the complete fragmentation of a team, who individually had so much to offer, but somehow could not work together. It was only through reflection on these incidents, and dealing with the casualties from them, that it emerged more clearly than ever that for the patient to receive the best possible care, multi-professional communication needed to improve.

The experience of working as a nurse abroad gave me a greater insight into how this could happen. The different interpretations of roles encouraged me to stand back and ask: 'Was it any better this way? What were the advantages for the patient and the team?' This was further augmented by my increasing clinical focus in critical care, where the need for multiple sources of expertise to manage a complex patient was explicitly obvious. As the nurse caring for the patient, experts actually came to ask me about the patient as part of their information-gathering for diagnosis and treatment. Why was I so shocked to be asked directly? Had my role as a nurse not always been important to managing the care for that patient? Why was I surprised that my interpretation of the patient's situation was valued? Why had it not happened before, and why had I not made it happen?

On reflection, it was clear that this was not just about me, but about professional cultures and established social practices, steeped in the legacies of the past, and a long-standing misunderstanding of different professional roles. It also made me question what other valuable sources of information I might have missed in caring for my patients. The richness of knowledge and expertise from the patient's friends and family, through to the most expert medical and therapeutic interventions was enormous, and communication was the key to unlocking it.

Formative events that I look back on in my career nearly always involved successful and genuine collaboration. However, they were often not achieved without painful moments along the way. If you truly believe in collaboration, it helps to keep you going, even when team members may be obstructive and unhelpful. I have learnt now to pause and really try hard to imagine what is driving the response, and what is colouring my perception. The difficulty today is that with increasing pressure on services and practitioners, we are often too ready to react and feel compelled to adopt a 'fire-fighting' approach to decision-making. In this time-competitive environment, time to reflect *in* action is scarce.

In the field of education and practice, the challenge is how to prepare future practitioners for multi-professional collaboration. There is a real need to demonstrate actively the skills of good teamwork and multi-professional communication, and to expound the benefits for patients and services. Perhaps the answer is to raise the profile of collaboration, both in the classroom and in practice. It could now be key to contextualise the successes and failures of collaboration, enabling each generation of professionals to build on what has gone before, and hence improving practice. For example, working within a multi-professional module team has had inspirational moments for me, including a refreshing enthusiasm for multi-professional education.

However, the problems of practice do not escape education. From my own experience, just getting the whole module team, with competing commitments, to one meeting was a logistical challenge. The importance of a stable team for successful collaboration has implications for the way we organise work patterns and student placements. More rotational posts are developing in an attempt to recruit staff and develop their breadth of experience. However, we must be careful that opportunities for a sustained contribution to a thriving team are not lost in the process.

At first, many students get frustrated about learning process-orientated skills. These sorts of skills are often taught in our initial multi-professional modules, with some students seeking more concrete facts and absolutes to know and learn. They do not always see until later – as I did not when a student – how valuable process skills are in professional practice. This includes how to present information to others; co-working on projects; debating an issue; critically appraising evidence, and the multiple of perspectives involved in shared problem-solving. Students seem to be under constant pressure to find the 'content' that they need to know. Perhaps that is partly the fault of the way we measure student success and educational outcomes, and it is an issue to consider as professional practice and education evolve.

In my experience, teaching multi-professional groups is fascinating, as the different perspectives really open out debates. Sharing of differences and similarities does need careful facilitation, such as when contentious issues arise and uni-professional factions form almost subconsciously. Perhaps it is a basic human need to belong to a group or a culture, but let us hope that it will be a multi-professional culture focused on meaningful health- and social care. It is tempting to want to look into the future, and to ask if this the best way to achieve change, and we need to exercise some patience in order to find out with any certainty.

I believe a culture of multi-professional collaboration will contribute to significant change, but this will become apparent only when *all* professions interact regularly in practice and in the classroom. In this way, I feel sure that by actually having the time to listen to each other's perspectives, we may come to understand more about one another's roles and motivations.

Thinking time: learning by doing

1 What, for you, are the key points about multi-professional collaboration, highlighted by this account?

a _____

b _____

c _____

2 How is this person's account similar to, or different from your own experiences?

3 Does this account raise any advantages or disadvantages of multi-professional collaboration?

- For the patient?

- For the service?

- For the employer?

- For the health- and social care professions?

Forward planning: using this book as a series of 'signposts'

Consider how subsequent sections in this book may help you to gain a fuller picture of the issues raised in this account.

So, what is multi-professional collaboration?
Section B Understanding the Nature of Collaboration
See Chapters 4, 5 and 6.

But what is there to be gained from working collaboratively?
Section C The Benefits of Collaboration
See Chapters 7, 8, 9 and 10.

But how feasible is multi-professional collaboration?
Section D Preventing Collaboration
See Chapters 11, 12 and 13.

What do you actually have to do to work collaboratively?
Section E Demonstrating Collaboration
See Chapters 14, 15, 16, 17 and 18.

CHAPTER 3

A Physiotherapist's Account

ICHOSE PHYSIOTHERAPY AS MY FUTURE CAREER at the age of 15, when I attended a school careers evening and was impressed by the kind of work physiotherapy appeared to offer. One of the perceived attractions of the profession I wished to join was my impression that physiotherapists worked fairly autonomously with a client on a one-to-one basis. This opportunity to help someone recover from injury or disease appealed to me. Subsequent work experience and investigation confirmed my initial interest, and I was accepted to study physiotherapy and subsequently qualified as a chartered physiotherapist.

When I reflect on those years of training, I have no memories at all of any mention of teamwork, or any real information about or insight into the roles and responsibilities of any other members of the health- and social care professions (dates with medics apart!). In fact, one of my early clinical experiences provided a very negative taster of collaboration.

During the early part of my training, having spent six months in the academic setting, we all had to undertake four weeks' ward experience, carrying out a range of duties such as making beds, assisting with bed-baths and bedpan rounds. It was my first real opportunity to see the healthcare team at work, but I am sad to recall that, with the exception of very painful feet, my most abiding memory of that experience was being told to hide in the sluice when the consultant did his rounds, so that

I wouldn't make the place 'look untidy'. Teamwork at that time, at least in the ward environment, appeared to involve doing what the consultant told everyone else to do!

Having qualified, like most new practitioners, I took a junior position in an NHS hospital, which would offer me the opportunity to work in a range of clinical areas over a period of one to two years, consolidating my basic skills. During this time I worked in an out-patient department where, being on a one-to-one basis with the client, teamwork and collaboration is minimal. I enjoyed this period of professional socialisation as it allowed me to concentrate on developing my own professional skills.

However, I also experienced work in an intensive care unit and on the neurology rehabilitation wards, and discovered that I could not work with the client in glorious isolation from the rest of the nursing, therapy and medical staff. I experienced, through examples of both good and poor practice, that not only do clients receive a better quality of care if the healthcare team works together, but also job satisfaction increases for the professionals involved.

As my experience of teamworking increased, I became more and more certain that my future career path must be in an area where I had the opportunity to develop collaborative care. So it was ideal timing for me when I saw a new post advertised that involved liaising with local general practitioners in order to set up and develop a new community physiotherapy service. The new base for this service was sited within an existing community office shared by community occupational therapists, and speech and language therapists. Fortunately for me I got the job.

This existing community service was already working successfully as a team, and had collaborative networks with nursing and health visiting. I was made to feel welcome immediately, and learnt much from observing colleagues and looking at their models of practice. They assisted me in developing the physiotherapy department as a service in its own right, and encouraged us to be part of the collaborative healthcare team. The benefits of this could be seen in the service the client received: for example, in the efforts made to undertake multi-professional assessments so that clients had to undergo only one set of questions and examinations, and also in holding case conferences that identified aims of care for the team and responsibilities for action.

My personal experience of the most effective collaborative care has been in the community setting, when the hierarchical nature of some hospital-based care does not exist and the client is placed at the centre of the decision-making process. Possibly my worst experiences have been there too. It is awful to stand with a client and their family in the family home and observe health professionals disagreeing with each other over how to manage the client's care. It certainly does not give the client and their family confidence in the service they will receive.

From this background I entered the world of education, first as a student teacher, then as a lecturer teaching on an undergraduate physiotherapy programme. All of us in healthcare education roles are aware of the pressures of trying to equip students with sufficient knowledge, skills and professional attitudes to be competent practitioners. At the same time, healthcare education is also striving to develop problem-solving and critical-thinking skills, so that practitioners can continue to develop as individuals and enhance their profession.

In order to meet the needs of the professional bodies, the universities and the students, many courses concentrate solely on the skills and knowledge of the specific profession, with minimal awareness of the role other professionals play until students undertake clinical placements. Other programmes aim to provide a more multi-professional perspective by teaching different student groups together; by sharing projects and assignments, and by encouraging a team approach to client management.

My experience in multi-professional education is that students do not automatically see the relevance of sharing teaching and learning about other healthcare professionals. They have made a career choice and now want to concentrate on achieving their goals without being diverted by what can appear to be blind alleys. Education is just like life, in that although we learn from what people tell us and what we read, we learn a lot more from observing what people do. We may teach students in mixed professional groups in either the academic or the practice setting, and describe good practice to them, but they will actually learn most from their observations of what happens in practice.

If we are to be successful in promoting collaboration at any level from undergraduate to postgraduate, it will be because students and qualified staff see examples of good practice that improve client care; demonstrate better use of resources, and give greater job satisfaction. They will want to emulate these examples of good multi-professional practice.

My journey to collaborative working has had its difficulties, and if I had been pre-warned, some of these problems could have been avoided. It was with this in mind that I welcomed the opportunity to be one of the authors of this book, so that the knowledge I have gained can be used by others.

Thinking time: learning by doing

1 What, for you, are the key points about multi-professional collaboration, highlighted by this account?

   a _____

   b _____

   c _____

2 How is this person's account similar to, or different from your own experiences?

3 Does this account raise any advantages or disadvantages of multi-professional collaboration?

   • For the client?

   • For the service?

   • For the employer?

   • For the health- and social care professions?

4 Can you identify any recurring theses across all three accounts?

Forward planning: using this book as a series of 'signposts'

Consider how subsequent sections in this book may help you to gain a fuller picture of the issues raised in this account.

So, what is multi-professional collaboration?
Section B Understanding the Nature of Collaboration
See Chapters 4, 5 and 6.

But what is there to be gained from working collaboratively?
Section C The Benefits of Collaboration
See Chapters 7, 8, 9 and 10.

But how feasible is multi-professional collaboration?
Section D Preventing Collaboration
See Chapters 11, 12 and 13.

What do you actually have to do to work collaboratively?
Section E Demonstrating Collaboration
See Chapters 14, 15, 16, 17 and 18.

SECTION B

UNDERSTANDING THE NATURE OF COLLABORATION

CHAPTER 4

Multi-Professional Collaboration: The Context

....

TAKING AN INFORMED APPROACH to multi-professional collaboration requires an awareness and appreciation of its context. By that we mean that collaboration does not simply appear out of thin air, but is embedded in and shaped by the prevailing policy agendas or 'drivers' of the day. There are many social, political and professional drivers, which are moving multi-professional collaboration up to the forefront of contemporary health- and social care initiatives.

This is not to say that there has previously been no collaboration, or that collaboration in itself is the panacea for all the problems facing the provision of health- and social care today. However, partnership and co-operation between different professional groups, services and agencies are seen as the most viable way of delivering the quality health- and social-care provision now expected by purchasers and consumers (Glenn, 2000).

UK examples of this have been a series of government directives in the last decade calling for health- and social care professionals to work together more closely for the benefit of clients (Miller *et al*, 1999). This has been echoed in the directives from each of the health- and social care professional bodies. These social policies and guidelines for professional practice influence multi-professional initiatives directly and indirectly, and will be discussed further in this chapter.

The framework for practice and multi-professional collaboration

The importance of a multi-professional approach to health- and social care, where all professionals who contribute to a client's care and therapy work not just alongside each other, but 'inter-professionally' to provide a seamless service, is unequivocally documented (Department of Health, 1989; Department of Health, 2000a & b; Griffiths, 1988). The aim of a multi-professional approach is to maintain and improve continuity of care as clients move from hospital to the community, and is a feature of the changing emphasis of health- and social care provision. Also, 'seamless care' involves developing a clear plan for the future health- and social care provision for each individual client, which is to be welcomed.

Demarcations and hierarchical relations between professions familiar with hospital-based services were neither sustainable nor appropriate in a community context (Barr *et al,* 1999). New ways of working had to be found that crossed preconceived boundaries to respond more flexibly to the needs of clients on their own terms in situations that the professionals could no longer control (Barr & Waterton, 1996). Also, based on recent political and demographic trends, it became clear that no one profession could provide adequate care for an increasingly ageing population who were more likely to live longer with multiple pathologies (Cameron & Masterson, 1998).

In order to support these changes in practice, the UK government's education and training directives also highlighted the need for more shared learning between the health- and social care professions. Although the prediction was that those who learn together might work together more readily in practice, thus delivering better total care, there is as yet little evidence to substantiate this. Logic and common sense might suggest that this is true, but as yet it is not an evidence-based initiative. Teamwork in healthcare has a long history, but as Leathard (1994) maintained, there has been little research evidence to substantiate the view that collaboration leads to improved quality of care that has furthered the wellbeing of clients.

From personal experience of teaching first-year pre-registration students together in mixed professional groups, it appears to be a valuable way of enabling students to appreciate different approaches to client-centred practice. Developing mutual understanding of the different team roles from an early stage during education might help to reduce the degree of uni-professional socialisation that has been very clearly documented as a strong influence in all professions (Freidson, 1994; Melia 1987). (See also Chapters 13, 14 and 17.)

The scope of practice and changing professional roles

The UK legislation (Department of Health, 1990) that created independent hospital trusts, general practitioner (GP) fund-holders and community trusts and one-tier practice led by primary care groups (Department of Health, 1997a) has produced radical changes in the organisation and delivery of care (Miller *et al*, 1999). The implications of this are a move to reduce the number of different healthcare professionals in contact with clients, thereby reducing the size of healthcare teams and promoting continuity. The consequence of this is that knowledge of each other's role and function becomes even more important within the diminished healthcare team.

Other apparent policy trends influencing practice include:

• Emphasis on evidence-based practice that has encouraged the development and implementation of guidelines for good practice in managing a wide range of conditions. The effective use of guidelines and 'care pathways' requires coordination and communication between the health- and social care professionals in drawing up and operating the pathways.
• The Patient's Charter (1999); the NHS Performance Indicators, and other quality initiatives raise patient expectations about the standard of care they can expect to receive. Such initiatives raise the profile of the patient in collaborative care.
• The introduction of multi-skilling of healthcare workers, with a consequent overlap of inter-professional boundaries, creates both opportunities for development and flexibility, as well as posing a threat to professional autonomy.
• The changing role of health- and social care professionals, which includes the delegation of some work to healthcare assistants, the take-up by nurses of some work formerly carried out by junior doctors, and the advent of nurse practitioners, and nurse and therapy consultants.

- Earlier discharge of patients from hospital, placing the emphasis on community care and good liaison between primary and secondary health carers, with subsequent changes in staff roles.

However, there is concern about de-skilling, and that multi-skilling inevitably leads to a dilution of skills. Here, the concern is that a 'generic' worker does not achieve the unique skills and level of expertise of the different professions. Ultimately, this could diminish the positive benefits

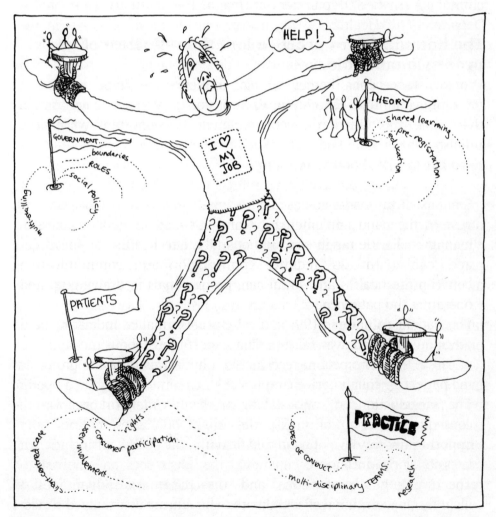

Figure 1 *The 'drivers' influencing and shaping multi-professional collaboration*

of 'multi-disciplinary' teamwork (Craik *et al,* 1998). This is particularly an issue in the context of chronic shortage of staff – particularly nurses, but also allied health professions (AHP) and general practitioners (GPs). Current problems in staff recruitment and retention have highlighted this even more in recent years, with healthcare organisations such as the NHS facing the crisis of how to manage services and meet a range of patient needs with fewer staff. Flexibility is essential, but concerns reign about accountability in a climate of defensive medicine and the introduction of clinical governance (Department of Health, 1997a, 1998).

The boundaries of practice and the influence of professional bodies

Our own professional bodies can also influence the shape and pace of multi-professional collaboration. Each professional group is accountable to its particular codes of conduct or ethics, and the way multi-professional collaboration is described and defined may provide both possibilities and restraints for collaborative working.

For example, the code of professional conduct for nursing and midwifery dictates that nurses and midwives 'must work co-operate with others in the team', defining the 'team' in broad terms to include the client, the client's family or carers, and other health- or social care professionals (NMC, 2002). So here providing care *is* recognised as being a multi-professional and multi-agency activity that relies on good teamwork and a sense of shared responsibility. Essential to this is interpersonal communication and inter-professional cooperation, based on mutual trust and respect. (See Chapters 15 and 16.)

The rules of professional conduct for physiotherapists emphasise this need by stating that 'physiotherapists shall communicate and co-operate with professional staff and other carers' in order to optimise the therapeutic interventions for the client (Chartered Society of Physiotherapy, 1996). Comparison with the code of ethics and professional conduct for occupational therapists sees an emphasis on respecting other professions and the pragmatic advantages of collaboration to ensure well coordinated and effectively delivered services (College of Occupational Therapists, 2000). These codes of behaviour are important: they influence professional practice and shape the nature of multi-professional collaboration.

The drive for collaboration and its benefits are less explicit in the Duties of a Doctor, which contains 14 key principles that guide the medical profession in their practice (General Medical Council [GMC], 2001). The majority of the principles reflect the doctor-patient relationship, but the Duties do contain aspects of multi-professional working by advocating that doctors should 'work with colleagues in a way that best serves the patients' interests'. It urges doctors not to 'discriminate unfairly against your patients or colleagues and you must always be prepared to justify your actions to them' (GMC, 2001). This implies at least the fundamentals of collaboration, and alludes to the importance of dialogue and effective communication in order to act in clients' best interests. An increased sense of the prevalence and value of teamworking is reflected in the core statement of professional values and responsibilities for good medical practice (GMC, 2001). This statement contains sections on working with colleagues, including working in teams and treating colleagues fairly. (See also Chapter 17.)

It is clearly impossible for any one profession to possess all the knowledge, skills and resources needed to meet the total healthcare needs of society. Quality care and effective service provision should be the product of a good team, and these aspirations may be encapsulated in clinical guidelines, position statements, or standards for practice. Professional frameworks that have previously guided the shape of practice may come under increasing pressure to be revised and updated in order to produce a more contemporary form of accountability. If the scope and nature of practice is changing, then supporting professional infrastructures needs to be both responsive and flexible, not archaic and unwieldy. However, it is still possible, and indeed it is paramount, for an individual practitioner to act with ethical integrity, especially if the issues surrounding multi-professional collaboration continue to be complex and demanding. 'Our old professional frameworks are no longer a suitable vehicle to deliver the type of care that is expected and needed. But, if any of us are to be successful transformational leaders, then our first step is to transform ourselves' (Gough, 2001).

Preparing for the future: commissioning multi-professional education

In addition to UK government policy and professional requirements, agencies such as the NHS Executive (NHSE) produce guidelines to purchasers and providers of education. For example, the UK government paper *The Health of the Nation* (Secretary of State for Health, 1992) pointed to the need for partnerships between individuals and organisations for the improvement of healthcare. Also, *Targeting Practice* focused on alliances to provide multidisciplinary solutions supported by multidisciplinary education (Department of Health, 1993).

During the last five years, the NHSE education and training planning guidance has consistently emphasised shared learning and multi-professional teamwork. The responsibility for the planning and commissioning of education and training has devolved from regional health authorities to local education consortia, and has evolved further into Confederations. The NHSE defined the future work of the commissioning body to include promotion of 'shared learning to support teamworking across professional and organisational boundaries, preparing the healthcare workforce to provide a coherent service within a primary care led NHS and across health and social care boundaries' (Department of Health, 1997b).

Interestingly, these guidelines were not directed at medical or dental education. The message was clearly to give impetus to the commissioning of shared learning, to improve and support multi-professional teamwork, and to create a common language to facilitate integration (Miller *et al*, 1999). The English National Board for Nursing and the Central Council for Education and Training in Social Work published a joint strategy for shared learning, which pointed to the ideal for healthcare consumers to receive integrated services to meet their needs, rather than being prey to professional boundary maintenance (ENB & CCETSW, 1992). This very real issue of professional 'tribalism' is referred to later (see Chapter 13).

Collaboration: multi-professional learning and working

The Standing Committee on Postgraduate Medical and Dental Education has produced a working paper for consultation on multi-professional working and learning (SCOPME, 1997), and a final report with recommendations in 1999. The working paper was based on consultations and written evidence across a number of health professions. It presented views on organisational and educational contexts for multi-professional learning, which it says has: 'entered a new phase which is about preparing practitioners to operate within a multi-professional context in the clinical environment. This approach requires a new set of skills centering on how professionals interact with one another in the clinical environment – how professionals form teams, how they plan together and make decisions together within the clinical context.' (SCOPME, 1997)

This paper makes a specific point about the skills needed to operate in a multi-professional team, citing forming teams, planning and decision-making as important generic concepts and differentiated from profession-specific theoretical knowledge. It concludes that: 'the time is now right for some principles to embed a multi-professional approach into systems for health care delivery and medical and dental education.' (SCOPME, 1997)

In the final report (SCOPME, 1999) it is interesting to note that the acquisition of teamworking skills is not seen as an explicit learning objective. Here, the assumption is that students can more effectively learn the appropriate collaborative skills 'on the hoof' and in a practice setting: 'A skills training approach in team working is neither necessary nor appropriate. If individuals are provided with autonomy and a climate of equity and mutual respect between different professions is created then a multi-professional group will develop its own ways of working and learning effectively together.' (SCOPME, 1999)

The paper refers to the need for practical examples of the experiences of multi-professional working. Clearly such examples could provide useful educational material, providing vivid illustrations of the realities of collaborative teamwork, which could engage and inform learners and novice practitioners (see Section E).

Whatever the educational arguments for common curricula (and there are many), the economic arguments are equally compelling (Mackay *et al*, 1995, cited in Barr *et al*, 1999). The heavy capital investment necessary to produce the learning materials can only be justified for large student cohorts and for curriculum initiatives delivered over a sustained period of time. It could be argued that any large-scale initiatives are counter-productive if the aim of multi-professional learning is to have the time and opportunity for meaningful inter-professional sharing. Economies of scale and pressures of time may mean that multi-professional learning initiatives are catapulted into existence, rather than nurtured and developed incrementally.

The research agenda: the driver of evidence-based practice

Another influence on the configuration and delivery of multi-professional collaboration is the need for health- and social care research and the drive towards more evidence-based practice. One of the priority areas in the nationwide research agenda is multi-professional education and multidisciplinary research. This again provides an attractive avenue for practitioners to advance multidisciplinary practice through collegiate research. Such collaborative projects can have a better chance of getting funded in today's climate of diminishing research budgets, while still meeting the increasing demands for evidence-based practice. Perhaps this may also provide a way for practitioners coming to know and understand each others' roles better if they participate in research together – an example of learning by doing: 'Collaboration creates new ways of being, doing and knowing' (Sullivan, 1998).

As uniprofessional education comes under closer scrutiny, so too does interprofessional education, from its own exponents and, increasingly, from the external environment (Centre for the Advancement of Inter-Professional Education [CAIPE], 1996). Educationalists feel that it is timely to substantiate claims that inter-professional education influences practice positively, and thus to justify the additional investment needed to build an interactive dimension into at least some of the occasions when professionals learn together (Barr *et al*, 1999).

Collaboration: a process between individuals

To conclude, the context of collaboration needs to be considered in the light of your own professional skills, values and attitudes, and with an understanding of what you as a practitioner can contribute. Your contribution will undoubtedly be shaped by what is actually possible, given the changing scope of practice and the various drivers influencing multi-professional collaboration. These key aspects are considered in the next two chapters, and in Section C.

However, the impetus for multi-professional collaboration is very much part of the current socio-political context, providing a continuing challenge for the individual practitioner and, as Glenn (2000) concludes in a Keynote paper: 'whatever the policy directive or organisational structure, the fundamental building block of collaboration and partnership relies on the relationships between people. Collaboration and partnership is a process which occurs between individuals, not institutions, and only the persons involved ultimately determine whether or not collaboration and partnership occurs.'

Summary of key points
- There are government directives that call for greater collaboration between health- and social care professions.
- This is echoed to varying degrees by uniprofessional codes of conduct.
- Educational providers have also responded to this call, although the evidence base that this will improve collaboration in practice remains sparse.

CHAPTER 5

Multi-Professional Collaboration: The Concept

WHEN TRYING TO TUSSLE WITH the notion of 'collaboration', it is certainly useful to have an understanding of the socio-political backdrop (see Chapter 4). This provides some sort of contextual 'map', so that those new to collaborative working can navigate their way through the turbulent seas of change, to become acquainted with what has gone before and what is driving the current changes.

However, part of the bewilderment of keeping abreast with new initiatives within health- and social care is trying to understand what everyone is talking about. So much becomes encapsulated in a key phrase or term ('evidence-based practice'; 'client-centred practice', and 'clinical governance', to name but a few) that it becomes almost a code or short-hand for a raft of ideas and concepts that need deciphering to make any real sense for practice.

Terminology: clarity or confusion?

'Collaboration' is also evidently one of those words that is used so freely and often and in a multitude of ways that it can become so generic and multi-purpose as to be reduced to a bland 'buzz word'. Although it can be instructive to have an 'umbrella' word that conveniently clusters many related ideas around a central tenet, it could be that such a term tries to embrace too much diversity and does not clarify, but instead confuses. Why complicate something that was clear to you before?

It may seem that there is no need for this chapter at all, but the issue that needs to be addressed is how collaboration is defined and described, and why those conceptual parameters keep evolving. Previous authors have remarked on how complex the notion of collaboration is (Henneman *et al*, 1995), and indeed 'collaboration' has been used to

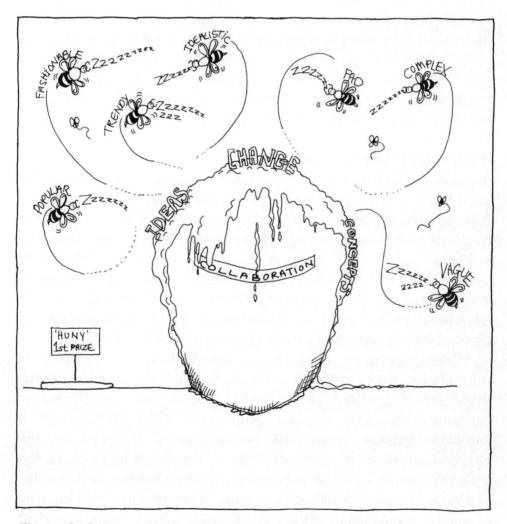

Figure 2 Collaboration as a 'buzzword': clarity or confusion?

describe practice at a range of service and organisational levels, including pre- and post-qualifying education (Barr, 2000; Dewar, 2000; Fitzpatrick, 1996; Nugent & Lambert, 1996). Given this context, you could ask yourself why it is worth bothering at all, as trends can be transient and everyday practice continues, regardless whether or not you use the 'right' terminology to describe it.

However, in this process, practitioners may feel devalued and uncertain, as if their experiences and insights do not really 'fit' into the current super-shiny ultra-modern health- and social care idiom of the day. This is a sad loss as practice requires innovation, implementation, consolidation and evaluation to progress, so everyone is needed and can make a contribution. Perhaps in looking at how 'collaboration' is described and defined, we can discover more robust ways of dealing with and adapting to change, so that we all develop more confident ways of integrating useful new ideas into our current working practices.

Defining collaboration

Beginning at the beginning, the simplest definition of collaboration is that it is about 'listening to, and learning from, others' (Davies *et al,* 2000). As Braye and Preston-Shoot (2000) point out, this can mean collaborating with service-users as well as colleagues. Onyett (1997) widens the net by including team members, users and carers as the key players in collaboration, whereas Dewar (2000) extends it to include clinicians, managers and government agencies. Other facets of collaboration entail the emphasis of working across traditional health- and social care boundaries (Reeves, 2000a) and across a range of agencies (Horder, 1996).

Other aspects of collaboration seek to define the outcome of collaboration: for some authors, it is the notion of the 'seamless, needs-led service' (Barr, 2000), or to provide more integrated care (Nugent & Lambert, 1996). Therefore, any definition of collaboration needs to encompass various strands – the people involved, the place and the intended outcome. If interwoven, these 'threads' help to make the definition more substantial: collaboration is about working with a range of different people, possibly across a range of organisations, and this way of working should manifest itself in discernible differences for individual clients, and possibly for the service as a whole.

Defining multi-professional collaboration

However, collaboration is not a word used on its own, but is frequently attached to a variety of prefixes. Most common is 'multi-professional' or 'multidisciplinary' collaboration, although collaboration has also been described as being 'interprofessional' and 'trans-disciplinary' as well. Each prefix has its own inherent subtleties: 'multi-professional' generally ring-fences the notion that collaboration involves not one, but a number of individuals from different disciplines. In contrast, the terms 'interprofessional' and 'trans-disciplinary' endeavour to depict more the method of working – namely that collaboration requires different professionals actively cooperating to achieve an agreed client- or service-focused goal. 'Transdisciplinary' collaboration is yet further on, describing the process of working together as one where skills and information are openly pooled and shared, and traditional professional barriers are blurred in order to deliver individualised high-quality care (Hickling, 2000).

Some authors have gone further and described collaboration as a 'synergy', implying that it is a dynamic process involving a multi-professional team that work interdependently to achieve a quality 'holistic' outcome (Gage, 1998). This does not mean to say that multi-professional collaboration is either compulsory or better, but different from outcomes that might be achieved with clients uni-professionally. You may be tempted to throw up your hands in horror, or be reaching for your dictionary in bewilderment, but perhaps the word 'synergy' is a more up-beat, energetic noun than 'collaboration', which often prompts rather negative connotations associated with wartime fifth columnists and subterfuge (Henneman *et al*, 1995).

Describing collaboration

It is possible to devise a taxonomy or classification of nouns and adjectives used to describe collaborative practice (see Table 1) and, indeed, you may well recognise some words used in other contexts to describe an organisation, management structure, or a way of working. An argument could be raised that collaboration is essentially about good teamwork, and therefore all attempts at arriving at a watertight definition are pointless. The reason that the endeavour to 'name and frame' the means and manner of collaboration persists is that it seems to be appreciably more than just the effective organisation of a team (Horder, 1996), or good team morale (Barr, 1997). Therefore, it is understandable that practitioners, educationalists, theorists, authors, managers, politicians and service-users continually endeavour to pin down and put under the microscope the 'what, why and how' of collaborative working.

With so many different perspectives involved, it is not surprising that the term most commonly used is the one that is the most generic and 'all-purpose', 'multi-professional'. Pirrie (1999) raises this issue of 'the continuing debate on terminology', and although the context in this case is education, the point is equally pertinent for healthcare practice. Pirrie goes on to conclude that, in the main, most people tend to use the most general term ('multi-professional') as it is the most ambiguous: 'one must adopt the term which gives the most room for manoeuvre'. Although the act of defining and describing practice is difficult to clarify, in some cases it feels as if the goal-posts of good practice are constantly moving and remain always just out of reach. Table 1 illustrates the vocabulary of collaboration.

Table I *The vocabulary of collaboration (positives and negatives)*

Association	Conspiracy
Co-agency	Cliquism
Confederation	Collusion
Cooperation	Patronage
Coordination	Merger
Consensus	Clannishness
Consortium	Polarity
Consultation	Contention
Joint working	Conflict
Synergy	Competition
Teamwork	Rivalry
Partnership	Opposition

Collaboration in practice settings

So, how would we recognise multi-professional collaboration? In the end, it is not the language we use to describe practice that is important, but that quality healthcare is being delivered, and that working practices are functioning to ensure and improve outcomes (Dewar, 2000). Patronis Jones (1997) describes collaboration as being manifest in a multi-professional approach to implementing client care. This includes all stages of the treatment process, from planning and consultation, to delivery and monitoring outcomes, and devising standards for practice, as exemplified by joint assessments and care pathways.

Certainly a central focus seems to be an agreed goal as well as a shared vision or philosophy of care, both of which entail co-ordinated planning in the short and long term (Fitzpatrick, 1996; Miller 2000). Nugent and Lambert (1996) saw the manifestation of collaboration as a shared approach to data collection, problem identification and assessment of clients to produce more integrated care. This requires not only shared decision-making within a team, but also effective multi-professional communication and a mutual understanding of roles, and professional and legal responsibilities. This comprehensive approach to working can lead to further collaborative ventures, such as joint commissioning for strategic development; multi-agency approaches to training, and multi-professional research initiatives (Braye *et al*, 2000, Onyett, 1997).

To ensure that collaboration is a true synthesis of different professional skills and client-focused action, all members need to feel included and involved. An ethos of sharing power and working with one another can prompt and sustain collaborative ventures (Braye *et al*, 2000; Gage 1998). Although it is neither possible nor feasible to encapsulate collaborative practice into a neat and orderly timetable, the time factor is a key issue. Dewar (2000) saw collaboration as 'substantial working together', and this underlies the commitment and energy required to initiate and sustain a collaborative venture, seeing it through from beginning to end.

The 'mindset' of interdependency

However, this can all make collaboration sound like very hard work, and a practitioner may feel at a loss as to where to begin. Gage (1998) suggests that a new 'mindset' is required, shifting the focus of practice from uni-professional independence to multi-professional interdependency. Also key is the attitude of the individual practitioner or practitioners; a positive approach to innovation, and being able to contribute to team morale. Headrick *et al,* (1998) put this blend of personal characteristics into a simple framework: 'A place to start is the fact that most health professionals have at least one characteristic in common, a personal desire to learn, and that they have at least one shared value, to meet the needs of their patients or clients'.

Perhaps one should add here that an additional shared characteristic is the desire to do a better job so that a patient or client feels consulted, cared for and treated as an individual. Given this starting point, collaboration may open up possibilities never previously explored, in terms of who you collaborate with, where and why. This can make collaborative practice a creative and occasionally surprising way of working that has implications for both personal growth and professional development.

'In their own words': practitioners' views of collaboration

'Collaboration is not competing with other professions, but being able to educate each other about our similarities and differences.'

'Collaboration is about cooperation and fostering an attitude of willingness to listen, learn and adapt.'

'Collaboration is about needing to know "the bigger picture" and the remit of your colleagues, including senior management.'

Tapping into 'a reservoir of potential'

The constituent features of collaboration are discussed in further chapters, which explore both the benefits of and the obstacles to working together (see Section C), as well as undertaking a more detailed examination of collaborative behaviours (see Section E). This chapter has set the scene and explained the concept of collaboration as a way of working. It is clear that collaborative practice is no picnic, and can be challenging in terms of time, resources and human endeavour. It is not an enterprise to enter into without support from colleagues, service-users and managers: you need allies and like-minded people in order to identify, plan and deliver successful collaborative projects.

An appropriate point to end on is to step back from inter-professional collaboration and consider how the world of work in general is changing. Zeldin (1999) comments on how technological advancement does not hold the key to everything, particularly within the realm of human relationships and people having time to communicate meaningfully with each other. Zeldin advocates new and creative ways of working within healthcare to enhance stimulation and expand our horizons, tapping into what he terms 'a vast reservoir of potential going to waste': 'We also need to invent jobs which exercise a greater variety of the lobes of the brain and more strings of the heart and which incorporate breaks and diversions into other fields. Without such breaks creativity cannot be sustained, the most effective way has been by bringing together people who have never realised what they have in common, and different kinds of work which have never known what they could achieve in combination'.

Summary of key points
- Collaboration is a broad term, used to describe the integration of working practices across a range of settings.
- Specifically, collaboration involves three interwoven strands of the people involved; the context, and the intended quality outcomes.
- Collaborative working is characterised by a shared vision, collective goal-setting and a mutual understanding of roles.
- Collaborative working also entails an ethos of power-sharing, and a commitment of time and effort.

CHAPTER 6

Multi-Professional Collaboration: The Individual

HAVING CONSIDERED THE WIDER context that has influenced the move towards multi-professional collaboration, and examined some key concepts, it is appropriate to consider one of the crucial elements in collaboration – the individual. The individual could be any health- or social care professional or worker, client or carer working collaboratively in any setting.

By definition, any interaction that is termed collaborative includes more than one person (or individual). Each individual has specific personal and professional beliefs, values and attitudes to bring to any interaction. This then is where potential problems can arise, as different, potentially conflicting, individual beliefs and values are brought to bear on a particular clinical decision that requires consensus.

Being aware of our beliefs, values and attitudes is seen by some as the key to being able to work cooperatively within the context of a multi-professional team. Not only do we need to be aware of what past and present influences shape the way we think and behave, but also how we can adapt and change: 'If we are all signed up to creating a health service which places the patient at the heart of it, we have to break down the traditional barriers and find new and flexible ways of working. To do this we need to change attitudes' (Gough, 2001).

Belief systems and our view of the world

Each of us has our own set of beliefs on which we base our way of life and our behaviours. The beliefs we have are wide-ranging and of differing importance. For example, your spiritual beliefs or the belief that you are loved and well regarded by your family may be central to your view of life. Evidence of these beliefs will be observed in your interactions and behaviours. Other beliefs, while sometimes vehemently argued and

Figure 3 Belief systems and our view of the world

debated, are not as central to your sense of self. An example of this would be your belief in which is the best football team, or the belief in the rights and wrongs of eating meat.

In 1968 Milton Rokeach categorised the belief-system into a hierarchical pattern based on the assumptions that:

- Beliefs are not of equal importance
- The more central beliefs are slow to change
- If a centrally held belief is altered, it has a powerful effect on the individual and their whole belief system.

The most centrally held beliefs are what Rokeach termed 'shared primitive beliefs'. These are the kind of beliefs that the majority of us share – such as that the Earth is round and orbits around the Sun. These beliefs are impervious to change, unless challenged by irrefutable and undeniable evidence. If this belief were shown to be incorrect, this would have a major impact on the certainty of other belief structures, and could lead to deep-seated insecurity and mistrust.

The second most centrally held beliefs are non-shared primitive beliefs. These beliefs are inextricably linked to how we see our particular world, and in the determining of what we value. An example of this kind of belief would be spiritual beliefs, or the belief that the people you call mum and dad are actually your parents.

One can only imagine the feeling of devastating uncertainty if a major belief on which you base your life is shaken or disturbed. A topical example here is the current protocols and accepted practices concerning adoption. Most people who adopt a child are now encouraged to be open about the circumstances of birth, with access to the child being easier for the natural parent or parents. However, the advancement of biological science has produced a modern-day situation, highlighting how central beliefs shape our view of ourselves. For example, it is reported that children who have been born using some of the assisted-conception techniques utilising donor eggs or sperm may suffer long-term anxiety. This may in part be due to being unable to trace their biological parent, thus being denied the opportunity to discover their 'true' identity.

Authority beliefs and their impact on working practices

Another category of beliefs concerns our views of authority, which are influenced by people whom we perceive as having authority over us. These may include our parents, teachers, managers, religious figures, and politicians. In health- and social care, this authority extends to practitioners with whom we work, or to lecturers in the academic setting. These authority figures shape our beliefs throughout our lives, but also offer the opportunity for us to challenge those beliefs as we develop our own individual personalities and characteristics.

Therefore, it is likely that authority beliefs will change over time, depending on the relationship with the authority figure. This may be a cause of stress or conflict, as it may be difficult to challenge someone in authority whom you feel you ought to respect and offer unquestioning compliance. Also, challenging a person in authority offers a threat not only to their beliefs about healthcare, but also to their status and power within an organisation.

Derived or inconsequential Beliefs

Derived or inconsequential beliefs are those we acquire from others with whom we identify. These may be people with whom we work or socialise, or people whose work we read or practices we adopt. What is interesting about derived beliefs is that they can have 'a halo effect'. This is when we adopt less important beliefs to another totally different area. It is reasonable to copy a particular physiotherapy technique and believe in its efficacy because it is favoured by a colleague for whom you have high regard. It is not reasonable to be swayed by that person's beliefs on whether one film is better than another, as that is not their realm of expertise. Another example is using celebrities for advertising. It would be understandable to adopt a particular coaching programme or team formation based on information from a famous footballer, but why believe that they know which is the most effective deodorant?

Inconsequential beliefs are the least strongly held beliefs, and change frequently throughout our lifetime. Change often occurs through individual experience; for example, the belief that the food at one restaurant is better than that at another. If these beliefs are changed, there is no profound effect on the belief system. It is accepted that such non-essential beliefs will change over time and with different experiences.

Beliefs are the basis from which we substantiate our values, and from these we develop our attitudes and behaviours. This is true in our working, family and social lives. So from where do we obtain our belief systems?

Formation and change of belief systems

The central shared beliefs are those that are inculcated by our whole culture, lifestyle and knowledge. We learn from our parents, teachers, peers, and our own experiences. We all acquire this information and experience as human beings, and therefore these beliefs are shared. The central non-shared beliefs are also gathered from our parents, culture, lifestyle and experience, but these will be different for each individual, based on the particular belief and value system of the culture, the individual's parents, authority figures and the experiences of the individual.

Authority beliefs are developed from our experiences with authority figures. These beliefs depend on many factors, such as the perceived power of the individuals involved and the feedback these people give to us, be it positive or negative. Even if an individual actually does not agree with the beliefs of an authority figure in a particular area, the strength of the influence can still be strong and persuasive. You may disagree with a particular belief your mother had over a parenting issue, but when you become an adult and a parent yourself, you may suddenly find yourself uttering the same words and making the same responses, and thinking, 'I sound just like my mother!'

Derived and inconsequential beliefs are acquired from many sources, and these vary with age and with different lifestyles and culture. For some people, their siblings' views may influence beliefs in childhood, teenage years, or throughout a lifetime. In teenage years, we are strongly influenced by our peers and by the media, by what our favourite television personalities and pop stars like/dislike and appear to believe in.

It is apparent that we all have a complex system of beliefs based on our culture, family, lifestyle and experiences. From our belief system, we decide what we value and this is termed our value system. A value is described as the relative worth you place on a particular item, person or experience. 'Values give our personal, professional, and collective lives structure, direction and meaning' (Clark, 1994). Values that are developed from our centrally held beliefs, particularly the non-shared primitive beliefs, tend to be important to us and relatively unchanging, such as the value we place on our spiritual beliefs, or the value of time spent with our families. However, the values we learn from other parts of the belief system are more likely to change over time and with experience and in a given situation.

Motivation and needs

Dr Abraham Maslow described a hierarchy of needs in 1954, which has been discussed and debated ever since. While the theory is not without its critics for being over-simplistic, it does offer an understandable and well-developed argument for the motivations underlying our behaviours and values. It also explains why we can react differently in a given situation depending on the context, because the same situation can have different values or outcomes.

For example, a young attractive woman receives a proposal of marriage from an elderly, attractive and rich man whom she likes, but does not love. The value she places on this proposal is not high and she declines. The same situation could occur to the same woman, but on this occasion she has just discovered she is in huge debt. His attributes and hers have not changed, but the context has. The value she puts on his proposal has risen, and this time she accepts the proposal.

Our first basic needs, and the ones on which we place most value, are physiological needs: the requirement for food, water and sleep. Once these basic requirements have been met, our next need is for security, and this means a safe place to live. The majority of us in the Western world often take these first two levels for granted, and do not place much value on them unless they are threatened. Consider how the perceived value of a job increases when threatened by redundancy. Redundancy has the potential to reduce or destroy a person's income and security, threatening the adequate provision for the physiological needs of any dependants.

Once physiological and security needs are met, we seek to belong to a group like a family or friends, and to receive positive regard from others. Through the lower three levels we seek to gain self-esteem, which can be described as the value we place on ourselves. While the factors that lead

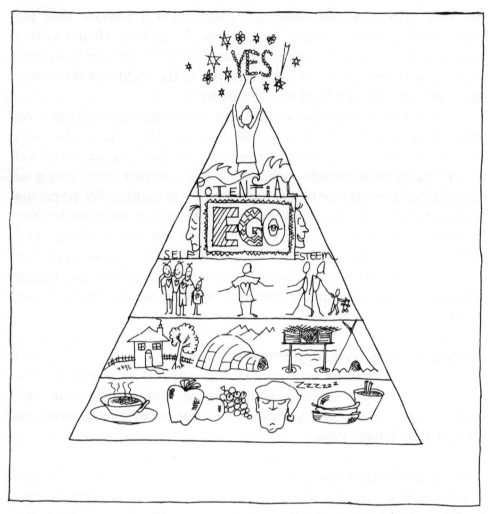

Figure 4 A pictorial representation of Maslow's hierarchy of needs (1954)

to a high level of self-esteem are many and varied, it is obvious that self-esteem is not fixed, but varies with different situations and changes throughout a lifetime.

Self-actualisation is the final and highest level of Maslow's hierarchy, and the level to which he feels we all aspire. The form that self-actualisation takes varies, but is based upon us achieving our own potential. Much discussion over the hierarchy has centred on whether individuals move through the levels in a progressive manner, or hop from one level to another. However, the levels are less relevant than the influences of a specific context. For example, if you were offered a drink in a pub but got only a glass of water, you might feel a little disappointed. But if the glass of water was offered to you in the middle of the desert, you might feel overwhelmed with gratitude.

In summary, individuals evolve their own value system, based on their beliefs and shaped by the specific situation. The goals or objectives that are valued in a situation are based on individual characteristics and a belief of their own self-worth. Given this complex intertwining of individual and workplace beliefs and values, it is perhaps not surprising that conflict can and does occur in teams. Values have been cited as one of the potential sources of conflict within teams (Mailick & Ashley, 1981; Mizrahi & Abramson, 1985). Sands *et al* (1990), in their paper on conflict in the interdisciplinary team, describe the need for, among other things, a common value base that transcends the boundaries of the different disciplines.

Attitudes: positive or negative bias

An attitude is described as a positive bias towards or a negative bias against, something or someone. Attitudes are derived from our belief and value system. An attitude is made up of three parts or components (Secord & Backman, 1964):

- The cognitive component
- The affective component
- The behavioural component.

The cognitive component is the categorisation and organisation that is involved when adopting an attitude. If asked what your attitude to 'glopas' was, you might feel you had no attitude to it at all, as it is a fictitious word with no real meaning. However, the word 'Oxfam' might trigger positive or negative feelings, as this is a recognisable word and associated with such concepts as 'charitable organisation'. Therefore, in order to have some sort of bias, you need to be able to recognise and categorise the person, object or situation.

Once categorised, you are able to identify the second component of attitude – the affective component. This is your emotional response to whatever you are considering. It is based on factual knowledge, experience and the values you hold. Therefore, if you are well informed about the work of Oxfam, you may feel a generally positive attitude. This may well be demonstrated by a third component of attitude, the behavioural component. For example, you may donate to Oxfam on an occasional basis or even work as a volunteer, depending on the strength of your attitudes, values and beliefs.

The cognitive, affective and behavioural components of attitudes tend to be complementary, and as individuals we prefer it if what we know, what we feel and how we act are consistent. If components are dissonant with each other, this can result in a feeling of unease and the need to justify the incongruity (Festinger, 1957). Take, for example, a person who knows all the facts about smoking and the negative effects on health, but who continues to smoke. This individual will justify this by offering examples of people who have smoked for 50 years with no ill effects, or will declare they can stop smoking at any time in order to dispel this dissonance.

Attitudes tend to be relatively fixed, but can change if the cognitive component is altered by new facts and knowledge, or the affective component is affected by experience. If a client has a negative view of male nurses, because they consider them to be less caring, due to a particularly extreme example in the popular press, this could be altered by facts that demonstrate a more realistic portrayal in the media, or a positive experience of having been treated by a male nurse. The behavioural change would be from avoidance or refusal to be treated by a male nurse to acceptance of treatment by a healthcare professional, regardless of gender.

Although an appreciation of the context and concepts underpinning multi-professional collaboration is useful, we ought not to overlook our own individual beliefs, values and attitudes. It is easy to get caught up in the 'bigger picture' of health- and social care, without paying due attention to how we are monitoring and interpreting our own experiences. We each have our own set of beliefs, values and attitudes. These are manifested in the way we behave to other people, and pervade all aspects of our working lives. In order to be self-actualised health- and social care practitioners, and enhance our continuing professional development, we need to cultivate insight and self-awareness.

Self awareness and reflection

Self-awareness is your personal judgement of your own worth. If we are self-aware, we are able to look at our attitudes and values objectively, and accept our limitations. We are able to identify not only our general strengths and weaknesses, but also the unique talents that we bring to a given situation. It should allow us to identify our own needs and short-comings, and to accept the contributions of others with equanimity.

Self-awareness is not innate, and can be developed by acquiring skills and abilities that are strengthened by being practised. It is important to consider not only what we do, but how we do it. The key here is not to wallow in mistakes and boundless guilt, but to broaden our repertoire of effective coping strategies for a myriad situations. This can be achieved in a number of ways.

- By receiving and valuing comments from others (feedback)
- By appraising our own actions in terms of what we did (performance)
- By reflecting on our actions in terms of their effects on other people (reactions)
- By appraising our actions in terms of what we actually achieved (outcomes)
- By considering environmental influences and their impact on what was possible (physical setting, social and cultural context)
- By considering temporal influences and their impact on what was feasible (past history; need to prioritise, and demanding time-schedules).

In working collaboratively, if we are self-aware we can identify our own skills and determine the unique contribution we can make to the attainment of common goals in order to maximise the benefits to the client. Refining reflexive skills and becoming a more reflective practitioner need not be a solitary endeavour, and is greatly enriched by talking with other colleagues (Clouder, 2000). Even if this is done briefly and somewhat 'on-the-hoof', the sharing of experiences, ideas and insights often has more vibrancy and meaning if related to an immediate event and practice setting. The scientific rationale of collaborative working can be guided by social policy, service objectives and workplace standards, but the art of collaboration may be best learnt by exploring what is happening within ourselves.

Summary of key points
- Any collaboration is as a result of a relationship between individuals.
- Each individual brings their own beliefs, values and attitudes to the collaboration.
- We each need to develop self-awareness, so that we can view objectively our own contribution to collaborative working.
- We need to be open to considering other peoples' beliefs and values that may influence their attitudes and behaviours.

SECTION C
THE BENEFITS OF COLLABORATION

CHAPTER 7

For the Client: Putting the Person First

THE BENEFITS OF WORKING collaboratively for a client shine through all the profusion of literature, theories, concepts and social policy directives: collaboration can produce a better quality outcome for the individual recipient of a service, treatment or therapy. At the heart of healthcare collaboration is a regard for the wellbeing of the individual client or user, and concern that a service or intervention should reflect personally relevant needs and individual lifestyles. To work collaboratively as a health- or social care team therefore entails continual consultation with patients or clients, and also conferring and negotiating with appropriate colleagues, services and agencies to make client-centred care a reality. These client-centred values for health- and social care can be reflected in the social policies and organisational agendas of the day, though genuinely affecting daily practice is more problematic.

This description of the benefits of collaborative working may seem obvious and simplistic. Client-centred care is the common humanistic value that binds professional collaboration together into a purposeful way of working, encompassing care, context, support and healing (Stewart *et al,* 1995). The clarity of this vision can often be shrouded in a plethora of terminology and debates about how to define client-centred practice or patient-centred care or, patient-focused care. This is complicated further by

Table 2 *An example of responding to client needs: the NHS core Principles (Department of Health, 2000c)*

- The NHS will shape its services around the needs and preferences of the individual patient, their families and their carers.

- The NHS will respond to different needs of different populations.

- The NHS will work continuously to improve quality services and minimise errors.

- The NHS will work together with others to ensure a seamless service for patients.

each professional group's own interpretation of 'patient' versus 'client', or even what constitutes a commonly shared and holistic view of 'health' (Fulford *et al*, 1996; Law *et al*, 1995; Laungani & Williams, 1997; Sumsion, 1999). This tends to highlight the preoccupations of the healthcare professions, seeking to define and protect professional boundaries rather than a regard for clients' needs and wants. (See Table 2.)

The concern with topical 'buzz words' and reinventing or reshaping fashionable concepts to fit timely healthcare trends can seem very remote from what is actually appreciated by an individual client or user. Collaboration can help to put the client first and foremost by enabling the efficient planning and delivery of integrated care, implemented with sensitivity and economy by the most appropriate practitioners and agencies.

Positive working relationships

If you ask a client about their experience of engaging in any sort of health or social service, or treatment, most will have an opinion on what was initially offered and what was actually received, and how they were treated as individual people. Over the years, the importance of the 'consumer's view' and opportunities to feedback and express opinions at informal and formal levels have become more apparent in the planning, implementation and evaluation of services. In other words, users of services have always had views about how they wish to be treated, but

Figure 5 'Excuse me, can I join in?'

found themselves in a situation where their views were not sought or taken seriously, or did not seem to prompt any real change.

An example of such consultation is that prior to the publication of the NHS Plan (Department of Health, 2000c). The opinions of 152,000 members of the public were sought before issuing a 'top 10' of commonly requested wants from a health- and social care service. To any health and social practitioner reading this book, the subsequent list ('top 10' requests) probably holds no surprises. (See Table 3.)

Table 3 *Seeking the consumer's views: an example of the public's 'top 10' requests (Department of Health, 2000c)*

1 More and better paid staff

2 Reduced waiting times

3 New ways of working

4 Care centred on patients

5 Higher quality of care

6 Better facilities

7 Better conditions for NHS staff

8 Better local services

9 Assured high quality treatment regardless of geography

10 More prevention and promotion of healthy living

Pared down to the bare bones, the benefits of collaboration can result in a positive working relationship where quality and attention to personal detail is as important as measurable gains in function, or the increase or reduction of medication. Becoming a recipient of a health- or social care service can be a bewildering, demoralising experience. It can mean the client having to redefine who they are and what the future holds in the light of a transient or persistent health problem. It means having to cope with uncertainty; feeling a loss of control over the direction of their life, and being dependent on others for practical or financial help.

Entering this world of being a healthcare 'consumer' may mean that they are required to do things for the purposes of diagnosis, assessment and treatment that may be embarrassing, humiliating and intensely personal. They may be surrounded by an unfamiliar world that appears to have its own indecipherable language. This world also moves at such a relentless speed that it is difficult to keep apace with the changes of personnel and frequency of events. At times like these, regardless of former attributes and life skills, the client can be at their lowest ebb emotionally and physically. It is then that they most need some sort of human contact and understanding, and to be able to make sense to what is happening to them (Mitchell, 1995).

A regard for interpersonal processes

The intricacies of being client-centred or person-focused arise when you consider that therapeutic human contact will be defined according to the individual, the personal style of the practitioner, and the interpersonal skills of both parties. For some clients or patients, being addressed by their preferred name is sufficient. For others, having the opportunity to give an account of their experiences to someone who has the time to listen is highly valued.

The timescale of the treatment or intervention is significant too, and what may be appropriate and timely for a brief and defined period may not be adequate over a longer period of continuing care. Here, the nature of the therapeutic encounter may need to be constantly redefined, and priorities re-examined within the context of an evolving relationship between client and practitioner. Given this wealth of variables, it is clear that there is no real 'formula' for client-centred practice that gives objective constituents or precise procedures that can be implemented with every client or patient. Therefore, the benefits of collaboration for clients and patients could best be described as interpersonal or social processes, which underpin the planning of treatment goals and the subsequent delivery of a service (Christensen, 1993; Sundeen et al, 1998).

These interpersonal processes are as much about the quality of the communication between the practitioner and client as about the outcomes or indeed the amount of time spent in any one-to-one intervention. This can encompass a variety of communication methods, including email, the internet, group meetings and case conferences, as well as verbal and written forms (Patronis Jones, 1997). The processes are essentially about the practitioner acknowledging the client as an individual person, and making opportunities to inform, include and consult the recipient of care routinely as treatment progresses, as well as at key decision-making stages.

If the person at the centre of the resulting care or therapy feels less of a mere number or name on a register and more like a real individual, then they are more likely to feel more positive about their future. Also clients are then more inclined to participate with procedures, and more willing to be actively responsible for their continuing health and wellbeing (Sumsion & Smyth, 2000). If a client is also clear and confident about how their treatment fits into a wider multidisciplinary context, and what the particular roles and responsibilities are of the professional team, then these positive benefits can be further enhanced. Given these positive gains, what have we got to lose? However, perhaps Laungani & Williams (1997) best illustrate the magnitude of this challenge: 'Patient-focused care involves more than adhoc surveys of patient satisfaction or an analysis of the activities that clinicians undertake during the care process. It is a radical realignment of the health service culture'

Partnership in planning and delivering services

Although acknowledging and involving the client to ensure person-centred care is a worthy aspiration, perhaps is does not go quite far enough in giving genuine influence and control to service users. Multi-professional and multi-agency collaboration can be an effective way of streamlining services to promote efficiency and to ensure that options offered are resourced adequately, thereby presenting genuine choice. Collaborative working can also be a constructive and creative context for exploring ways in which services are planned, monitored, reviewed and revised by both the users and deliverers of services. Opportunities to involve clients actively in planning and delivering services can often tread a delicate balance between being too *ad hoc* and informal, and being too constricted by protocol and procedure. Either extreme can be unproductive – either totally inconsequential or totally terrifying.

Perhaps it is more useful to see client inclusion in the context of a continuum. Arnstein (1969, cited in Jack, 1995, see Table 4) saw participation as a 'ladder'; at the very top rung sit citizen-control and user-empowerment, epitomised by socio-political frameworks that facilitate power sharing and equality. The very bottom rung of the ladder of participation is represented by processes that present users with false or illegitimate opportunities to be involved, such as being placated (being fobbed off) or manipulated (not being consulted at all).

If collaboration is truly about effective partnership between the client and a multi-professional or multi-agency service, then client inclusion

Table 4 *A client-centred approach, putting the person first (based on Arnstein (1969, cited in Jack, 1995)*

Being acknowledged – who am I?
- I am acknowledged by my name, age, gender and life context.
- People (professionals, workers) communicate directly and openly with me.

Being included – what is happening to me?
- I am informed about what will happen and what to expect.
- I am included in planning goals and prioritising actions.
- I receive and can readily use information and literature to inform my decisions.
- I feel I am adequately supported by people, facilities and appropriate agencies.

Being consulted – what decisions do I need to make?
- I am offered genuine choices and my preferences are respected.
- I am provided with opportunities to review and evaluate the service I receive.
- I can negotiate and discuss changes to my programme.
- I am aware of the anticipated outcomes of my treatment (timescale, effects).

must be evident in how a service is designed, delivered and subsequently changed. The true impact here is that a service team may need education and training to learn how to practise in a client-centred way, as well as contributing their time, skills and knowledge (Sumsion & Smyth, 2000).

The wider context of multi-professional collaboration is that the public is expecting far more from the available health and social services. Examples of this include the UK government's initiative such as the Patient's Charter (1999); the rise of user involvement and consumerist interest in service-planning, and active lobbying of disability organisations for social change. People today are better informed and more vocal about their rights, and the standards of care they feel entitled to expect (Pilgrim & Waldron, 1998). In the past, healthcare services and professionals could be accused of being too paternalistic, as typified by 'the doctor knows best' attitude. The impetus of user involvement initiatives is to redress that balance, and for service planners and implementers to take note that the client is the expert on their healthcare needs and wants.

True collaboration in practice would be a natural consequence of health- and social care services coming of age; where adult negotiations between a person with health needs and a service are epitomised by commonly held goals, and a freedom to effectively target and operationalise flexible and adaptable resources. This could be an empowering and energising vision of the future of health- and social care, but it is clear we are not there yet.

In the short term, there are immediate and obvious benefits to collaboration. The client can feel acknowledged as an individual person, and is involved and consulted regarding the content and process of their treatment. Although these benefits may seem modest and unambitious, the aims of collaboration in the long term could blossom if the growing culture of needs-led services and pro-active user involvement continues to thrive and inform social and political initiatives.

Collaboration: making small everyday changes

Such a long-term view of change may appear to be an excuse for accepting the status quo as it is, and an easy way of doing little in the meantime. The practitioner's responsibility to evolve collaborative practice could be seen as being no more demanding than optimistically waiting for the wider socio-political infrastructure to change the direction of service delivery, and allowing that to percolate down to day-to-day practice over time.

Although the legislative framework for collaborative practice could facilitate its development, the real seedbed of change lies within the attitude and approach of the individual practitioner and collective values of professional groups. It can be rhetorically impressive to talk 'big', but it is often far more meaningful to take action in small ways, and to strive to be 'client-centred' in everyday routines and commonplace procedures. For example, the NHS Plan (Department of Health, 2000c) acknowledged that a patient's experience of health- and social care services can be enhanced by initially addressing 'little things that improve dignity, comfort and convenience'. A practice illustration of the 'little things' approach is changes within a day centre for older people with dementia, which included the following (Kitchen & Stancombe, 1998):

- Allowing staff to eat meals with the clients to encourage socialisation
- Replacing teapots with ones that pour without 'dribbling' to promote clients' independence.

One of the fundamental conundrums of collaboration is that health- and social care professions are at odds to decide quite what being client-centred means, and if the benefits enhance or erode professional roles and identities (Dalley, 1999; Laungani & Williams, 1997; Sumsion & Smyth, 2000). These roles and identities have often been forged during times of rapid change and serious realignment of professional practice within increasingly varied contexts of health- and social care. It is probably not an exaggeration to describe this time of change as a battlefield, where professional groups have clung on to their existence and viability in today's health- and social care arena, and where there have been losses as well as triumphs.

Having survived this far into the new millennium, professional groups feel somewhat besieged on all sides, having to contend with government directives and policy, professional politics and local issues, as well as an increasingly articulate and expectant user-involvement movement (Barnes & Warren, 1999). It is not surprising then that professional groups and individual practitioners are unsure whether following a client-centred approach is the best and most logical move forward in improving the quality of care, or whether it is a retrograde step. The reticence is not always about the fear of losing professional power and control, or of being convinced that the practitioner does indeed know best and is the infallible 'expert'. The practitioner may feel an ambivalence towards honouring deeply held professional values about caring and respecting the personhood of others, and what may seem the contrary demands of overwhelming unwell, uncertain and demoralised clients with unnecessary information and poorly resourced or non-existent choices.

Establishing and maintaining a client-centred focus

The benefits of collaboration for the individual client can be stated in a few salient principles: a person would like to be acknowledged as a human being, to be involved and to be consulted about treatment or therapy as relevant to their needs and preferences. This requires teams to draw actively on the strengths of being multi-professional, pooling skills, knowledge and resources while retaining a client-centred focus. The five principles of client-centred care are listed in Table 5.

Table 5 *Five main principles of client-centred care (based on Laungani & Williams, 1997)*

1 Empowerment of clients/service users
2 Enhancement of staff (generic and profession-specific skills)
3 Multi-disciplinary integrated care pathways (mapping of entry to exit routes through services)
4 Multi-disciplinary teamwork (shared philosophy and collaboration)
5 Restructuring and decentralisation of services

Such principles appear deceptively simple, but it is within the historical, social, political and cultural context of health- and social care locally, regionally and internationally that the complexities of being truly 'client-centred' become apparent. Indeed, client-centred practice is not a new phenomenon as it has a track record spanning decades. 'Client-centred' was originally associated with therapy in the 1950s (Carl Rogers, 1980), and profession and service initiatives to implement core 'client-centred' principles have been developing since the 1970s and 1980s (Dalley, 1999; Stewart *et al* 1995; Sumsion, 1999).

The ethos of client-centred care needs to be grounded in day-to-day collaborative practice and the everyday experiences of clients. As the practitioner, you need to be willing to reflect on your current practice, which may entail critically appraising well-established ways of working and seasoned assumptions about how practitioners and clients should interact. However, being continually self-aware and self-monitoring can be a time-consuming and challenging enterprise (see Chapter 6). The remit must be that it is more than safely sanctioning what you do already, but paves the way to person-centred improvements for the individual client. Indeed, by addressing the 'little things' and making what may seem small, inconsequential changes to your practice, you may be actively contributing to the 'bigger picture' of a more caring and compassionate service. 'There is no professional territoriality when it comes to compassion, justice and respect for persons' (Kitson, in Fulford *et al,* 1996).

Summary of key points

- The benefits of collaboration can result in better working relationships and better quality outcomes for the individual patient or client.
- Collaboration requires the practitioner to actively use and sustain interpersonal processes with clients and colleagues in order to make client-centred practice a reality.
- Client-centred collaboration can start with small, everyday changes in practice.
- Client-centred collaboration requires the practitioner to be continually self-aware and the service to be responsive, flexible and open to change.

Action plan: Benefits of collaboration for the client: putting the person first

- How can you develop/enhance your understanding of client-centred care? Based on the SMART criteria of setting objectives (see Introduction, pxix), devise an action plan towards achieving a quality improvement in your everyday practice.

Personal/professional goal

Service/organisational goal

Thinking time: an opportunity to reflect on the value of a client-centred approach to goal-setting and service delivery

1 Being acknowledged as an individual person is a fundamental human need – you are more than 'just a student' or a designated professional role ('the nurse', 'the therapist' or 'the doctor').

Make a list of the services/facilities you use is a typical week, and see if you can recall if the following occurred:

- You were called by your preferred name and title.
- You were personally greeted or acknowledged in some way (by eye contact, shaking hands or a verbal greeting, such as 'hi' or 'hello').
- There was a brief exchange of pleasantries that seemed to set an appropriately receptive atmosphere (the day's weather, the latest news, the ease of any journey, locating the relevant department/reception/office).
- You were asked for your opinion or offered a choice of options.
- You had an opportunity to ask questions and to go over anything you did not understand.

2 Being client-centred may require you to acknowledge the client as an individual person at all stages of the treatment/intervention process. This needs to involve the client in the formulation of goals and being consulted regarding options and key decisions.

Think about your current practice and how you can actively acknowledge, involve and consult through all stages of a client accessing and using your service.

Are any changes:

- Definitely possible? (A positive 5)
- Possible with some work? (A sound 4)
- Just about possible if a major rethink were involved? (A hesitant 3)
- Not really appropriate at the moment? (A reluctant 2)
- Absolutely impossible? (An intractable 1)

Stages of accessing and using a service (score from 1 to 5)
1 Selection, choosing the right service
2 Entry, accessibility, referral systems
3 First contact, waiting lists, timescale
4 Assessment, negotiation of goals
5 Intervention, meeting clients' needs
6 Review, reassessment and review
7 Closure, exiting a service
8 Follow-up, continuing needs met, re-referral systems .

(Based on the flow-process model, adapted by Ovretveit, 1992.)

CHAPTER 8

For the Service: Effectiveness and Efficiency

THE AIM OF THIS CHAPTER IS TO look at possible and proven benefits of collaboration for service provision. The aims of a service or healthcare organisation may include intentions to provide high quality effective and efficient care in a variety of settings, and to a defined population with a variety of needs. Given such a wide remit, it has been extensively acknowledged that no single healthcare professional can provide for the total needs of the individual client. Consequently, due to the increasingly complex needs of clients and their carers, optimal care requires the coordinated effort of members of the multi-professional team. Government policy may provide a framework for such collaboration, as illustrated by national standards of care, with reduced demarcations between staff and removed barriers between services to provide faster and more efficient healthcare (Department of Health, 2000a).

This chapter will look more closely at the role of collaboration in enhancing clinical efficiency and effectiveness. Also considered is whether collaborative working can contribute to quality improvements in services, as well as simply addressing numerical gains, such as more clients seen by fewer staff for less money.

A consistent approach to service improvements

A starting point in this debate is to begin with the obvious. Logic would suggest that improved communication between the healthcare team would allow for quicker and more appropriate referral of clients to initial and subsequent services. Ideally, this could result in a more consistent approach to each individual's care, if the plan was agreed upon and communicated well within the multi-professional team and to the client. There are many successful examples of this in practice already. However, the very real impact of resource limitations can curtail services fully implementing or sustaining new and imaginative collaborative initiatives. A solution to this could be to look more creatively at the way we allocate and manage resources, and the evidence we use to underpin clinical decision-making.

Clinical effectiveness is related to quality service improvements in that it requires the questioning of professional activities and an active search for best practice. Dissemination of successful outcomes is necessary so that services that face similar issues nationally and internationally can benefit from a critical review of evidence and practice. Each service may have different contexts of care, and this needs to be borne in mind, but communication of good practice across agencies and organisations can provide working examples that investment of effort in one area influences practice in others. For individual practitioners within a service, a collaborative approach is likely to produce quality results by augmenting the clinical expertise and research awareness within the multi-professional team.

Multi-professional teams are being promoted in healthcare as the means to finding solutions to cost and quality problems. Boundaries are becoming less defined than in the past, with emphasis on collaboration and working together to provide an efficient and quality service. In the USA, rising healthcare costs have increased stakeholder interest in more specific outcomes of care that address not only a client's health improvements, but also wider psychological and socio-political problems. To this end, and together with the search for 'best practice', a system of outcomes management has been tried in different areas. The crux of this process is dependent upon multi-professional collaboration.

Multi-professional collaboration and managing outcomes

So, how do you begin to manage 'outcomes'? Remember that 'outcomes' has a very specific meaning in today's healthcare, and is intended to take us beyond vague intentions or hopeful aspirations. 'Outcomes' are measurable differences in an individual client's health and wellbeing, though specific target-setting is equally applicable for service planning and development. If outcomes are our real achievements and can act as indicators of our clinical effectiveness and efficiency, the process of outcome management can make an active contribution to quality improvements and enhancing practice.

The principle steps in the process of outcome management are the setting of outcomes for clients through collaboration, followed by review of literature and practices in order to define agreed multi-professional practice standards. The next stage involves implementation of those practices, with active education and role-modelling by practitioners. If followed by rigorous evaluation and audit, this can generate research questions, quality improvements and practice development opportunities culminating in the determination of best practice.

Outcome managers are needed to facilitate this process, as they need to acknowledge the importance of each discipline in the achievement of positive client outcomes. In order to develop meaningful standards for practice that are owned by all those involved in delivering the service, there needs to be discussion and agreement that acknowledges professional and philosophical differences, in order to distil best practice. Identification of common goals and client priorities is crucial to guide decision-making in practice and ensure cost-effective service delivery.

Wojner (1996) cites a successful case of outcome management in a Texas hospital with relation to the diagnostic related group of 'specific cerebrovascular disorders except transient ischaemic attacks'. Although practitioners were quite negative about the process initially, they demonstrated a reduction in length of stay, and readmission rates, with increased consultation between disciplines and increased patient satisfaction. These are clearly valuable service benefits. Not only does it allow for prediction of resource consumption and identification of quality enhancement targets, but it also empowers practitioners and promotes optimal client-driven care delivery. However, some of the benefits of collaboration are less tangible than discrete outcomes. These include greater understanding and willingness to cooperate within a multi-professional context, this being difficult to quantify and translate into 'hard data' such as percentiles and ratios.

Case management and contingency planning

There is evidence to suggest that similar concepts such as case-management do improve the service through formation of a focused, multi-professional team. McHugh and colleagues (1996) described how a multi-professional team used communication and collaboration skills to improve patient care on a busy surgical service to maintain continuity of care in the face of decreasing lengths of stay and increasing patient acuity. These issues are prevalent worldwide in healthcare, so there are valuable lessons to be learnt. It was also acknowledged that the best examples of collaboration occurred in the longest-standing relationships within the team, and so a core of stable members was crucial to the project's success. In striving for a collaborative relationship, each person was expected to contribute their perspective on the plan of care before reaching a decision by the group.

'Contingency planning' was also incorporated into the process of multi-professional collaboration, which allowed for agreed routes of action to be taken if different problems emerged for the client, allowing needs to be met without unnecessary delay for medical review. Decision trees or 'maps' were found to be useful in some situations. The shared accountability in case management for client outcomes worked for this team, who took a collaborative approach to trouble-shooting. When clients failed to progress as expected, this prompted team analysis and recommendations for service revisions, not recriminations or apathy.

Certain standards of care and expected outcomes have emerged from this process, which have helped to monitor and improve the quality of care delivered by the service. Flexibility with scheduling team-meeting or rounds at mutually acceptable times was key. Specifically, they created realistic and reasonable care plans, as well as organised and well planned care, resulting in a decreased length of stay and culminating in improved satisfaction for providers and patients (McHugh *et al*, 1996).

Outcome management and case management are not unique to one service or one client group, but they clearly generate universal principles that can promote good practice. These initiatives contribute to continual quality improvement, and reflect the benefits of multi-professional collaboration.

However, as an individual practitioner, you should not lose sight of your specific professional contribution to the team. Many of the care pathways used to map a client's progress through the healthcare system are task orientated or medically focused, not enabling retrieval of nursing data, for example (McCloskey & Maas, 1998). These authors also caution against 'groupthink', where collaboration really implies conformity and the abuse of power. They highlight this with respect to nursing in particular, where nurses may respond to conflict situations by using compromise and accommodation strategies rather than more collegial strategies of confrontation and collaboration (see Chapter 11). However, feeling undervalued and unheard within a team is an all-too-often recurring theme for any professional group that feels in the minority, or lacks the experience to equal the status and views of other well-established professional groups. True collaboration is not simply overwhelming dissenting views, or ignoring the need for constructive debate before arriving at an agreed viable consensus.

Meeting the challenge of service provision

Some of the challenges faced by community mental health teams in the UK have highlighted the need for collaboration in order to provide an efficient and effective community mental health service for a particular population, addressing any local, regional and national needs. From this example, the challenges subsequently identified encompass actions required at all levels and all interfaces of a service (Hannigan, 1999).

The key features of this list highlight collaborative principles of teamwork, discussion and agreement with shared standards, language and documentation. The need to communicate comprehensively and effectively is a common strand that unites all of these elements (see Chapter 15). In view of the profound structural, financial, organisational and professional problems in care coordination of mental health services, which are acknowledged by the government (Department of Health, 1997c), it is remarkable that multi-professional services are being provided to some clients successfully. Clearly, without organisational and strategic collaboration, service provision is in danger of becoming increasingly

Table 6 *Multi-professional collaboration, challenges for service provision (based on Hannigan, 1999)*

* Team aims, priorities, target client groups and boundaries
* Team membership, and roles and responsibilities of professional groups
* Eligibility criteria for access to services
* Agreed client pathways to and from care
* Unified models of case management and care coordination
* Standardised documentation
* Compatible information technology systems
* Shared standards for the exchange of information and the protection of client confidentiality
* Agreement over role as team leader
* Agreed management and accountability systems

fragmented. Collaboration offers opportunities for multi-professional development, multiple accountability and equality among partners in care.

Many current quality assurance activities in healthcare are still profession-specific, and not sufficiently client-focused (Ovretveit, 1994). Methods for improving collaborative working enable teams to identify quality improvement issues and their part in the process. This in turn empowers a team, enhancing their confidence to resolve issues rather than resort to professional in-fighting and negative criticism with no constructive effort. Mapping client pathways through a system can help a team to identify pitfalls in the process, where communication breaks down and possible solutions can emerge with dialogue and better understanding of each other's roles in the process. This enables staff to set standards or reveal processes that are too complex and need redesign, thus improving the service to clients (Ovretveit, 1994).

Quality healthcare and clinical governance

Government focus on quality healthcare has been embodied in a series of Department of Health papers, culminating in the publication of the *Clinical Governance Framework* (Department of Health, 1998). The key changes focus on:

- Cooperation replacing competitiveness
- Easier, swifter and fairer access to services
- Ensuring provision and regulation of high-quality services
- The importance of partnerships.

The policy aims emphasise that care should be provided in partnership between professionals and organisations, involving patients and the public in individual and service decision-making. These partnerships include:

- Health and social services will work with service users and the public at large.
- Health authorities will draw up health improvement programmes in partnership with local agencies.
- NHS Trusts will have a statutory duty to work together with local authorities.
- Local authorities will have a duty to promote economic, social and environmental wellbeing, and to develop partnerships with organisations including the NHS (Sealey, 1999).

Dewar (2000) highlights the professional implications of clinical governance, describing three levels of inter-professional collaboration where the implementation of common standards may occur:

1 At the level of managers, who need to accept that clinical governance represents a collaborative contract between:
   - The government
   - National Institute of Clinical Excellence (NICE). Collaboration between NICE, and relevant organisations and professional bodies, is intended to set national standards through research appraisal, dissemination of guidelines and facilitation of audit
   - Other local managers

- Professionals working to change and develop local services.

2 At the level of local healthcare economies, multi-professional teams will need to work across organisational boundaries to implement the National Service Frameworks (NSFs), focusing attention on standards of care for user groups – eg, for mental health services and coronary heart disease.

3 At the level of individual clinicians, healthcare professionals will need to collaborate, due to new mechanisms for standard-setting, and to apply increasing numbers of national clinical guidelines. The guidelines will represent substantial collaboration of scientist, politician, manager and clinician, and will have influence over clinical decision-making.

In services with a strong history of uni-professional standards and autonomy, collaboration must be nurtured and supported by many different stakeholders, rather than simply being prescribed nationally. Collectively, a network of new accountabilities may enhance the implicit power of all sectors of a service. This may also represent a significant culture shift, as services negotiate for quality improvements based on a common philosophy and shared values and beliefs.

Shifting the power base

From a service perspective, clinical governance provides a framework through which healthcare organisations are accountable for continuously improving the quality of their services. This can help create an environment in which clinical excellence in practice will flourish (Department of Health, 1998). Of the key themes within clinical governance, collaboration is central to most and the networks of accountability can help foster the culture of collaborative working that is necessary to achieve such objectives.

Accountability is needed to underpin the multi-professional collaboration necessary to deliver clinical governance (Dewar, 2000). It establishes the values within which work has meaning, and it enables formal assessment of action to achieve change. However, the complex reality of health- and social care today involves a network of intermeshed accountabilities. Accountability for achieving the standardisation of clinical quality rests as much with Trust chief executives and the work of the new national bodies NICE (National Institute of Clinical Excellence) and CHI (Commission for Health Improvement), as with individual professions and specialities. A framework needs to support the implicit power and authority of each group, in order to deliver effective clinical governance. Effective participation and appropriate organisational and personal development are required to sustain change. The NICE guidelines and constructive action-planning as a result of CHI inspection should all help organisations to get the culture right. Meaningful involvement of all participants in clinical governance means shifting the power base for decisions, particularly if significant involvement of the public in quality management is to occur.

The drive of clinical governance underlines the interdependence of all those working in a service seeking to provide better quality, client-centred care. The aim is to make services more responsive to clients' needs through representation from all stakeholders, and to facilitate an inclusive approach to service-planning. Strategies to increase quality care need to be evaluated in order to respond to changing service needs. Dissemination is then important to provide consistency and maximise the benefits across a service. However, equity of access to services, rationing of resources and taxation are key issues that impinge on delivery of quality improvements, and these are powerful cards to play in the political arena. Some assurance is necessary in order to convince clinicians, service users and the public that restructuring of services signifies genuine benefits, rather than paying lip-service to unattainable ideals to win transient political favour.

Summary of key points
- Collaboration by sharing information is essential to establish clinical effectiveness, efficiency and hence consistency across the service.
- Fundamental changes in the way we communicate across organisational, geographical and professional health- and social care boundaries are essential to improve service provision.
- Partnerships between professionals and managers, individuals and the organisation, and between the NHS, clients and the public, require successful collaboration to meet the clinical governance agenda.

Action plan: benefits of collaboration for the service

- How can you develop/enhance your understanding of the organisational implications of collaborative working? Based on the SMART criteria of setting objectives (see Introduction, pxix), devise an action plan to achieve a quality improvement in your everyday practice.

Personal/professional goal

Service/organisational goal

Thinking time: opportunity to reflect on the service gains of collaborative working

1 Identify what sort of forums exist in practice to discuss and plan service provision.

2 Who is involved in this process at any one time, and is there anyone or any viewpoint missing?

3 Are we utilising time efficiently to plan care, or is there an alternative approach you have read about, experienced or would like to try?

4 Identify what is already in place in your department and organisation to facilitate multi-professional collaboration.

5 What are the priority issues that you would wish to address if you had the opportunity to bring all parties together in one place to resolve a key issue? Do you think it would rank as equally important on their priority list? Why or why not?

CHAPTER 9

For the Employer: Job Satisfaction, Retention and Recruitment

THERE ARE FEW HEALTHCARE PROFESSIONALS, clients, managers or service providers who would argue with the benefits of collaborative care in relation to the experiences of the individual client, their family and friends, or with the potential benefits to the quality of the service provided.

However, subjective benefits regarding the individual's experience and empowerment are difficult to quantify. While quality of care can be measured by quality assurance mechanisms, such as waiting lists and patient satisfaction, employers are interested in what measurable benefits there can be in promoting collaborative care in the clinical setting. The benefits often then come down to economical measurements, in relation to cost-cutting and staffing issues. Economy need not be doing more for less (money, staff or resources); it is also about economy of effort and scale. Economy can be about what is prudent, sensible and value for money.

Potential cost effectiveness of multi-professional collaboration

Collaborative client care has the potential to be cost-effective. With staff working together there should be no duplication of services, and with the most relevant care being provided at the optimum time, treatment ought to be effective and therefore shorter in duration. With the various agencies and professionals working as a team, streamlining of care will take place with minimum delays in transferring or discharging patients. If the most appropriate care is provided initially, the amount of follow-up care should be reduced. All of these factors should lead to the most efficient use of resources and may result in cost savings.

Examples of government initiatives to support quality collaborative practice include the framework known as clinical governance, which aims to link efficiency (quantity at work) with effectiveness (quality at work) (Department of Health, 1998). Organisations need to be effective, and that means a prevailing climate of sharing, requiring trust and openness, as reflected in the following list of identified factors influencing organisational effectiveness (Northcott, 1999):

- Shared goals
- Shared culture
- Shared learning
- Shared effort
- Shared information.

This list embodies the essence of collaborative working. It provides a framework for practice that is ideologically sound and cost-effective. 'Interdisciplinary practice may not be the model for all settings, but it can be the most cost-effective model for greater patient satisfaction and better outcomes.' (Singleton & Green-Hernandez, 1998)

Enhancing job satisfaction

Job satisfaction may be described as a measurement of the level of satisfaction and achievement that people feel they gain from their jobs. It is an important issue for employers, as job satisfaction is linked to a lower rate of staff turnover and to greater productivity. This can have the knock-on effect of improving the quality of care that clients receive (Crose, 1999).

In seminal work, Herzberg, Mausner & Snyderman (1959) studied job satisfaction and found that the factors that lead to job dissatisfaction are not, as would be expected, the opposite of the factors that lead to job satisfaction. He postulated that the determinants of job satisfaction are the motivators or higher order needs of a job (achievement, recognition, responsibilities and advancement). However, job dissatisfaction is not merely the negative versions of these motivators, but factors relating to the lower order needs or 'hygiene' of the overall work context, such as working conditions, relationships with coworkers, company policy and pay. Although these 'hygiene' factors may reduce job dissatisfaction, they do not necessarily improve a worker's motivation to do well. For example, occupational therapists in the USA identified the following four key areas as contributing to job satisfaction (Okerlund *et al*, 1995):

- The amount of freedom within the job
- The opportunity to develop skills
- The salary and fringe benefits
- Positive treatment by coworkers.

It could be argued that one of the benefits of collaboration in the workplace is increased job satisfaction, as staff work more closely together as professionals, and also work more collaboratively with clients. The resulting teamwork should enhance job satisfaction. For example, an American study in 1992 (Ames *et al*) surveyed the satisfaction of all nursing service personnel in one medical centre (a sample size of 975). The results showed that the main factors linked with satisfaction at work were social interaction and open lines of communication. This included collaborating with members of the healthcare team during the process of making decisions concerning client care and service delivery.

However, job satisfaction encompasses a whole range of issues, which may be related to personal factors; factors related to the job itself, and factors relating to the organisation. It is therefore difficult to define, as it can only serve as a general indicator of 'psychological wellbeing' among staff (Health Education Authority [HEA], 1997). Although it can be measured, it can only provide a general barometer of staff attitudes and behaviours.

A survey was commissioned by the National Health Service Executive to look at health at work in the NHS. The report presents the findings from staff surveys in 14 NHS Trusts. Fifteen thousand staff were selected at random, and 8,500 responded. The level of job satisfaction reported by all staff groups appeared good, with the highest satisfaction being reported by dental, medical, nursing and midwifery staff. The lowest level of job satisfaction was reported by maintenance and works staff, although this group still scored well above the mid-point. The lowest available score was 1 and the highest 5, and the mean was 2.48 (HEA, 1997).

Job satisfaction is not a simple factor to measure, particularly in healthcare. In a recent study, Rose (2000a) measured overall job satisfaction for all kinds of healthcare employees. He reported a range of scores, with the average being 40 per cent. Nurses scored 39 per cent, while the most satisfied group were medical secretaries, with a score of 67 per cent; the lowest score was hospital pharmacists, with a low 13 per cent. The scores only demonstrate relative positions and do not describe at what level satisfaction becomes dissatisfaction.

One of the interesting results from the study is the finding that employees in relatively small healthcare organisations (under 25 people) are two or three times more likely to score above average in terms of job satisfaction (Rose, 2000b). It is conjectured that in a smaller team it is easier to create effective teamworking with a shared culture and common values that enhance job satisfaction.

Job turnover and multi-professional collaboration

If job satisfaction is viewed as an interesting, but not very scientific or measurable method of assessing the benefits of collaborative working for the employer, then job turnover may provide a more convenient measure. This may well be due to the fact that job satisfaction is not an accurate prediction of turnover. This would be supported by the results from the HEA study, which demonstrated a reasonable level of job satisfaction while at the same time retention continues to be a major problem for healthcare organisations, including the NHS.

Dissatisfaction may lead to job-searching and a renewed interest in the job advert pages of professional journals, but it may not lead to a staff member actually resigning (Spencer & Steers, 1981). The most striking feature when reading the literature that abounds on the subject of job turnover is the variety of vocabulary utilised. For example, turnover, instability, wastage, labour mobility, retention and attrition are just some of the terms commonly used in the literature. Due to these inconsistencies, the collection and comparison of data across studies is difficult, and complicated also by the range of measures used to calculate turnover.

Labour turnover, as characterised by voluntary resignation, can be costly in terms of both money and organisational disruption: 'the price associated with turnover rates is extremely high when the costs of termination, recruitment and orientation are considered' (Crose, 1999). It may highlight unfavourable comparisons with the external labour market or internal dissatisfaction with job content, working relationships or remuneration. Therefore, any lowering of turnover due to increased collaboration and working relationships is to be welcomed.

Addressing job turnover

While a high level of turnover is acknowledged to be an undesirable feature of an organisation, it must be considered that not all turnover is disadvantageous. New staff can bring fresh ideas, enthusiasm, knowledge and skills, so when measuring turnover it must be considered whether it could be termed functional or dysfunctional. Dysfunctional turnover would be classified as high-level turnover of experienced, high productivity employees in a market when that level of expertise would be difficult to replace.

For example, the NHS is the largest employer in the UK, with a workforce of approximately one million. Labour turnover has been recognised increasingly as one of its major problems (Buchan, Bevan & Atkinson, 1988). In 1999, the Department of Health conducted a survey of vacant posts and found that 7,285 posts (3.5 per cent) for qualified nurses and midwives had been vacant for three months or more (National Audit Office, 2001). The problem of dysfunctional turnover within an increasingly diverse workforce cannot be addressed easily by a single solution. Retention strategies need to employ a range of methods to retain staff, such as identifying turnover 'hot spots'; gathering data from well formulated exit surveys, and offering training and advancement opportunities (Bevan *et al*, 1997).

Recent figures show that the overall turnover rate for nursing staff in the UK was 12.3 per cent in the year up to March 2000, while the turnover rate for the allied health professions for the same period was 16.9 per cent. This includes a wastage rate (staff lost to the NHS) of 10.5 per cent (pay and workforce research, cited in Davies, 2001).

One of the most recent strategies in addressing the current shortage of staff has been to target trained staff who are no longer working within the NHS, and to encourage them to 'Return to Practice'. One multi-professional recruitment and retention group working in Oxfordshire has been effective in targeting, marketing and recruiting a range of professionals to return to practice programmes and into employment. This is a further example of collaboration, where a common issue is identified and a common solution devised. Working together the group were able to:

- Identify similar problems
- Plan local approaches
- Pool resources effectively
- Support and monitor the programme (Grout, 2000).

This example demonstrates how collaboration can be advantageous to a range of professional groups. With turnover being such an issue in current healthcare, it is essential that employers are creative and focus on ways to increase job satisfaction, thereby reducing the costs involved in turnover and recruitment (Crose, 1999).

Stress and burnout: a need for a multi-professional approach?

Other issues related to job satisfaction that could be linked to turnover are stress and burnout. Stress is a widely used term in society today. In the literature investigating the workings of organisations, there is much evidence to support the view that high levels of stress in the workplace can have adverse effects on the organisation in terms of job satisfaction and turnover.

Stressed therapists are being stretched to breaking point by ever-increasing workloads, inadequate staffing levels, and lack of time with patients (Ogden, 2001). The findings of this study of allied health professions carried out by the health unions also reported that only 6 per cent of those surveyed would definitely continue to work for the NHS (Ogden, 2001).

Stress tends to be studied uni-professionally, but even within professional groups, the identified stressors and reported stress levels vary. For example, a recent study identified a low level of stress in occupational therapists working in Sweden in comparison with higher levels of reported stress among English occupational therapists (Wressle & Oberg, 1998). As the stressors identified included specific work practices within the UK, occupational stress needs to be considered as both a workplace and cultural phenomenon. Much useful research could be undertaken to identify if there are stressors that are common to a range of, if not all, professions involved in health- and social care. By identifying common factors that lead to stress we may also identify effective coping strategies from which we could all benefit. 'Future research could examine inter-professional or intra-professional differences in terms of stressor frequency and stressor severity, and could evaluate the effectiveness of the coping strategies that they use. In this way, health professionals and managers will be better equipped to effect the most appropriate interventions to combat work-related stress among all levels of health service staff' (Laungani & Williams, 1997).

The relationship between stress and the syndrome known as burnout has been demonstrated in a number of professions, including health- and social care, and nursing. Burnout is defined as 'a syndrome of feelings of emotional exhaustion, depersonalisation and reduced personal accomplishment' (Maslach *et al,* 1996). It has also been described as a 'crisis of competence', resulting in professionals feeling a lack of confidence and ineffectiveness (Cherniss, 1995). It is felt that many health- and social care professionals whose jobs require prolonged and often demanding contact with clients can become emotionally drained and stressed beyond a capacity to cope.

The symptoms of burnout are increased effort but decreased productivity; mental and physical fatigue leading to distancing behaviour, and lack of flexibility in response, which leads to a proclivity to 'go by the book'. Evidence of large-scale burnout can be seen in behaviours such as high levels of absenteeism and high staff turnover. Nurses are considered to be particularly prone to burnout (Demerouti *et al,* 2000). According to two studies in Europe, 25 per cent of all nurses are affected by burnout (Landau, 1992; Saint-Arnaud *et al,* 1992).

Interestingly, one of the concerns expressed by the staff that can lead to stress and burnout is the pressure of expectations from clients (Hall,

After a holiday.....

Cool ~ no problem!

Slightly warm ~ no time!

Burning up ~ no control!

Burn out ~ no.....?

Figure 6 The burnout 'thermometer'

1994). While job satisfaction in healthcare comes mainly from the relationship with the individual client, this relationship has changed in recent years in relation to a number of issues:

• The rights of patients to expect certain standards of care. For example, The Patients' Charter (1999) and clinical governance.
• The rights of patients to access their own medical notes. For example, the Data Protection Act (1988).

- The change of emphasis of healthcare, from the passive recipient of prescribed care by professionals ('the patient') to person-centred and needs-led multi-professional service ('the client').
- The importance and measurement of outcomes.
- The increase in litigation.

If working in a more client-centred way results in practitioners perceiving that even more is expected of them, then multi-professional collaboration could raise the stakes yet again. In driving up expectations and, more significantly, the likely timescale for discernible benefits from collaborative working, team morale could suffer and initially enthusiastic staff 'burnout'. Burnout can lead to increased turnover, increased absenteeism or sick leave, and increased grievance, all of which are measurable for the employer and can be used as quantifiable evidence of success or failure.

Sustaining high-quality staff performance
There is much written extolling the benefits of collaboration for the individual client and for healthcare professionals. Employers are also encouraged to view collaboration as a means of achieving cost-effectiveness, increased job satisfaction, and the allied benefits of increased retention and recruitment. However, although it can be argued that mutual support and collaborative teamwork can act as a stress 'buffer', it can also raise expectations to unrealistic proportions. Clearly, what is needed is a multi-professional approach to the very real issues for healthcare employers: recruiting and retaining the right person for the right job, and facilitating a sustained high quality performance.

Summary of key points
- Effective organisations demonstrate the main characteristics of collaboration.
- Job satisfaction is multi-faceted, and therefore difficult to measure accurately. However, the level of perceived job satisfaction is determined by intrinsic aspects of the job, such as responsibility and recognition.

- Job turnover can be a major problem in healthcare organisations. Any approaches that may influence job satisfaction or stress in the workplace, and therefore reduce turnover, are to be encouraged.
- High levels of stress in a workforce have an adverse effect on any organisation. Stressors in the workplace across professional boundaries should be studied, and coping strategies identified.

Action plan: benefits of collaboration for the Eemployer

- How can you develop/enhance your understanding of job satisfaction or retention and recruitment issues? Based on the SMART criteria of setting objectives (see Introduction, pxix), devise an action plan to achieve a quality improvement in your everyday practice.

Personal/professional goal

Service/organisational goal

Thinking time: an opportunity to reflect on the employer's perspective of collaborative working

1 Consider your current service and identify any formal/informal protocols or integrated care pathways.
   - Have these protocols or pathways been audited?
   - If not, what can you do to influence this?
   - If an audit has been carried out, how has this influenced service development and a cycle of continuous quality improvements?

2 Identify a forum at work where important staff issues can be raised (not client-based):
   - Do you utilise this forum to discuss issues relating to job satisfaction/dissatisfaction?
   - Do you feedback to the appropriate level of management?

3 Westland (in Keable, 1997) claims that basically three personality types vulnerable to burnout can be identified. Do you recognise aspects of your working self in these descriptions?
   - *The dedicated worker* – takes on extra work on top of current caseload and responsibilities
   - *The over-committed worker* – works above and beyond the call of duty putting in extra hours, resulting in little or no social life
   - *The authoritarian worker* – believes that only they can do the job properly and refuses or is reluctant to delegate.

4 Self-awareness and being aware of how you react to pressure can be the key to spotting the initial signs of dysfunctional work stress (Westland, in Keable, 1997). Can you:
   - Describe your own personal signs and symptoms of stress? (Making avoidable mistakes? Losing or misplacing objects/equipment?)
   - Identify what sort of work stressors particularly affect you? (Tight deadlines? Presentations? Team conflict?)
   - Identify what resources in and outside work you can utilise to help you cope effectively? (Peer support, scheduled break, refresher course, new hobby or activity).

5 How do you take care of yourself and address your own needs? Covey (1989) sees balanced 'self-renewal' as one of the seven key habits of highly effective people.

In a typical week/month/year, what do you do to address your needs in these four dimensions?

a Physical (healthy living habits and life-style).

b Social and emotional (family, friends, social networks, membership of organisations and leisure activities).

c Spiritual (personal uplifts, renewal of values, meditation or prayer).

d Mental (reading, writing, continuing education and study).

CHAPTER 10

For the Health- and Social Care Professions: Core Skills and Professional Development

IN PREVIOUS CHAPTERS WE HAVE identified that collaboration within a practice can have benefits for the client, the service and the employer. If this is indeed the case, then why is collaboration not embraced more enthusiastically by health- and social care staff, and the professions these staff represent?

One reason may well be that professionals are continually having to deal with change and uncertainty. When individuals and professions feel threatened by many and various internal and external challenges, the tendency is to close ranks and look inward in an attempt to preserve the familiar status quo. Although this is understandable and a natural human response to change, it can become an automatic reaction to all new initiatives. This can result in fresh approaches to multi-professional collaboration being dismissed or ill-considered, without being properly evaluated. How does this happen and how can we address this?

The process of professional socialisation

Even those professions that are seeking to work collaboratively and multi-professionally are not in agreement as to how collaboration should be introduced and nurtured. Each profession has its own specific knowledge base, skills, code of practice and underlying philosophy, which leads to a particular culture and value system (Evetts, 1999; Kappeli, 1995). The expectation is that, as a student moves through the professional educational process, leading eventually to graduation as a qualified professional, they will not only learn and be able to apply the knowledge and skills specific to the professional group, but they will also take on the less explicitly articulated values, attitudes and norms of the profession. The process whereby a student moves through those stages of an evolving identity is called 'professional socialisation' (Sabari, 1985).

Professional socialisation occurs not only during formal education and training, but can commence during pre-education in work-shadowing or employment within a healthcare or social setting as a support worker. Observers also conclude that professional socialisation continues to occur when new graduates begin employment as qualified practitioners, acknowledging a transition from a novice to an established member of a profession.

A multi-professional dimension to professional development

Some argue that for students to absorb all the theoretical and practical knowledge required of them, and to meet the standards demanded in clinical practice within the educational programme, all the emphasis has to be on uni-professional issues and knowledge. Once practitioners have clarified their own professional role and identity, they will then be able and willing to embrace those of other professional groups. However, if professional groups concentrate only on their own uni-professional identities, they may become resistant to embracing the values and aims of other professions. This can give rise to stereotypical views of other professional groups that can become habitual and ultimately influence collaborative teamwork (Kamps et al, 1996).

Perhaps we need to pause here to consider what benefits there may be to the professions if collaboration occurs within the formative years of the educational process. It is clear from the requirements of being a professional that there is a unique body of knowledge linked to particular professions. However, it is also evident that there are overlapping areas of

Table 7 *Becoming a professional (Cohen & Sampson, 1999)*

Becoming recognised and accepted as a member of a professional group requires that the individual:

- Knows the conventions of the profession.
- Uses professional and technical language appropriately.
- Reflects critically.
- Applies the major principles and concepts on which the professional operates.
- Understands how relationships between theory and practice operate.
- Recognises ethical issues.
- Identifies relevant evidence and applies it.
- Works independently as an autonomous healthcare practitioner, as well as interdependently with multi-professional teams.
- Applies technology appropriately in practice.
- Is aware of the ideas and activities of professional associations.
- Participates in performance-enhancement activities.

theory, principles, skills and attitudes underpinning professional practice within the broad parameters of health- and social care. Finding common ground in the education process in such areas as critical reflection, evidence-based practice and ethical issues may help the development of a common professional and technical language. This would ease communication between professions, and would help clients who are often bewildered by the array of technical jargon. The development of a common language may also assist in the development of common objectives, promoting good practice and a providing a quality service to clients. (See Table 7.)

Acknowledging core skills and knowledge

Professions often feel that any sharing of knowledge will dilute their knowledge base and decrease the power they exert in the perceived exclusive ownership of this knowledge. But the converse view can also be argued. If common ground is identified and allows us to see what core skills we all share, it can also lead us to clarify what specialised, specific areas of knowledge and skill each profession has to offer. This will strengthen, not weaken, each profession's identity. By being clear and confident about our professional similarities, we can use more effectively our professional differences that are the unique 'trademark' of each distinctive professional group.

While professional groups may argue that they are already confident of their own specific contribution to healthcare, the same cannot be said of the general public's view of the health professions. An example of this comes from a study in 1996, which investigated perceptions of the physiotherapy profession. The authors stated that much of the work previously investigating the physiotherapy profession 'portrayed physiotherapy as lacking a clear identity: there is evidence of uncertainty in the public, and even healthcare professionals, as to what physiotherapists do; a failure to differentiate physiotherapy from other healthcare professionals' (Whitfield *et al*, 1996).

In the same study the authors suggest a generic term 'therapist' would be supported, as the group representing the public were unable to differentiate between categories of therapists, such as the difference between osteopaths and physiotherapists. It is not to the advantage of any of the professions to have such lack of clarity regarding their roles.

The role of education in professional development

While undergraduate education undoubtedly requires development of profession-specific knowledge and skills, it should also include the skills necessary for working with colleagues from other professional groups. Teaching and learning strategies that allow students to work together collaboratively can enhance professional development, as this gives them the opportunity to learn from experiences other than their own (Cohen & Sampson, 1999). This prepares students for the realities of practice today, providing them with a wider, more circumspect multi-professional context in which to examine and explore their own professional identity.

Candy *et al* (1994) stated that the undergraduate level of education should allow a broad view of one's own profession and an overview of how your own profession links with those of others. In other words, a 'helicopter view' of practice that allows for awareness and some understanding of how the professional groups, health- and social care organisations and client populations interconnect. Although this introduces students to the complexities of practice, it can also provide a more realistic 'map' of what exists, as well as spotting opportunities for change. However, another view argued is that until novice practitioners have clarified their own relationship to their profession and have sufficient clinical experience to be able to reflect on their own experiences, they are unable to benefit from the experiences of others (Pirrie *et al,* 1998).

A balanced view is perhaps the most persuasive in that, while each discipline has a need to develop grounding in basic knowledge and skills, waiting to introduce multi-professional collaborative working until after graduation is a missed opportunity. It could also be argued that collaborative skills and profession-specific knowledge could be developed simultaneously, helping to integrate practical experience from fieldwork or clinical education. 'Gradual and graduated opportunities – and time for reflection on the process of working and learning together – are essential ingredients of effective instruction' (Clark, 1997).

While there is debate about the inclusion of multi-professional education at undergraduate level, there is much support for this kind of education at post-qualification or postgraduate level. Pirrie *et al* (1998) investigated the perceptions of multidisciplinary education and stated that the subjects in their study considered that multi-professional education had greater impact at post-registration level, or at a late stage in the pre-registration curriculum.

The outcomes of multi-professional collaboration

While there is much support for the inclusion of multi-professional collaborative education, it is still unclear what topics or themes are best served by this approach, or what learning methods are the most effective. The drive for collaborative education is to help in the delivery of co-ordinated, cost-effective, high quality healthcare, which should have a direct impact on client care (Barr *et al*, 1999). Given all the variables, demonstrating a clear link between education and outcomes at practice level is difficult, but Oxman (1994) concluded that education could be linked to a 20–50 per cent change in a professional's actions. It could be argued, therefore, that collaboration at any level of education will enhance patient care, and in doing so, will enhance job satisfaction and the status of the professions involved.

Enforced collaboration as epitomised by external drives to economise or reorganise in either education or practice can be perceived as threatening to individual institutions or professions. Under threat, professional groups and services can fragment and be reduced to planning to stave off a crisis, and any opportunities for the cohesive development of collaboration may be restrained or lost. Pirrie *et al* (1998) recommended five principles as a way of promoting cohesive and collaborative multi-professional practice, as shown in Table 8:

Table 8 *Promoting multi-professional practice*

1 Make explicit the policy for promoting multidisciplinary education and practice.

2 Define terms used to describe various forms of 'multidisciplinary' provision.

3 Specify aims and objectives for each kind of initiative.

4 Convey strategic policy on multidisciplinary education to education commissioners by providing examples of good practice.

5 Recognise that effective multidisciplinary education requires more rather than fewer resources, and therefore adequate resources must be provided.

Embracing change

There has been an enormous amount of change within the health- and social care professions within the last decade, both nationally and globally. For example, the educational basis of many of the professions changed in response to the NHS reforms of the 1980s. *Working for Patients, Education and Training* (Department of Health, 1989b) encouraged cooperation between Regional Health Authorities and Higher Education institutions. Many previously NHS-based education programmes such as nursing, midwifery, occupational therapy and physiotherapy transferred into universities. Funding arrangements have changed: in 1997 the funding arrangements for degree-level nursing moved from the Higher Education Funding Council for England (HEFCE) to the Department of Health.

The Government paper *A Health Service of all the Talents: Developing the NHS Workforce*, published in July 2000, recommended that the funding streams for undergraduate medical education, post-graduate medical and dental training, and non-medical education and training should be merged. Regional directors would be responsible for effective workforce planning and development at all levels. How this will work in action is yet unproved, but if all the professional groups are to utilise these funding streams effectively and to the benefit of the client, collaboration must occur as client care is seldom uni-professional.

During recent years, the balance of healthcare has moved from acute care (secondary care) to primary care through the establishment of primary care groups and the development of their purchasing role (Department of Health, 1997a). The aim of this paper is to encourage seamless, coordinated care across sectors and demands that professions collaborate. How the health- and social care professions self-regulate has also come under scrutiny. For example, the government has expressed concern, on behalf of the public, over regulation of all the professional groups involved in care. The consultation document *Modernising Regulation, the New Health Professions Council* (Department of Health, 2000d), and subsequent documents look at developing a multi-professional regulatory body, which aims to 'protect the public, to support the development of a well-trained, modern, flexible workforce capable of delivering high quality, safe and effective care.'

The changes within healthcare policy and regulation that have been described are just some of the key changes to have impacted on health- and social care. What is clear is that, in times of change, individual professional groups, particularly the smaller professions, have a limited ability to influence government policy. Professional groups need to work collaboratively so that they can respond jointly to consultation documents; learn from each other's good practice and concerns, and allow implementation to occur in a coordinated way, so that both clients and staff suffer the least amount of disruption.

Continuing professional development (CPD) and lifelong learning

While all professional groups have engaged in some form of continued development and training post-qualification, it has tended to be variable in extent, content, availability and resourcing. Initiatives to forge a more cohesive multi-professional strategy for ensuring the continued competence of practitioners are evident, as illustrated by *The New NHS; Modern, Dependable* (Department of Health, 1997a). This is clarified at the organisational level, with the government seeing a clear correlation between quality of care for patients and ongoing professional development. It has been further developed in consultation documents on regulation of the professions, in which ongoing competence and fitness to practice needs to be demonstrated.

One method of demonstrating competency is the undertaking of continuing professional development (CPD) and lifelong learning. Different professions use the terms in differing ways, but for the purpose of this book they will be used synonymously to describe the process that professionals undergo to maintain, develop and enhance their skills, knowledge and competence in the workplace, and in preparing for future developments.

While some professions have always had to demonstrate evidence of ongoing education or training linked to competence, this has not always been the case for all health- and social care professions. However, with the increased prominence of profiling and portfolios as ways of providing evidence of professional development, the demand for continuing education has grown in recent years. While, for the process of regulation, it will be the individual practitioner's responsibility to demonstrate professional development, the objective is to enhance practice for the benefit of client care (Mills *et al*, 2001).

As previously discussed, much client-centred care requires a range of professional expertise, and so it would seem appropriate that much CPD should be shared across multi-professional groups. This is true not only for post-qualification and post-graduate programmes, which increasingly target multi-professional groups, but also for valuable, less formalised opportunities for CPD, such as in-service training, clinically based research and experiential learning. A real benefit of collaboration in CPD could be enhanced, evidence-based practice and research, leading to improved client-centred services (CSP, 2000).

Summary of key points

- Professional socialisation takes place over a prolonged period of time. If we are to develop teamwork in health- and social care professionals, they need to collaborate throughout the period of professional socialisation.
- Multi-professional collaboration can help us to identify core skills common to all professions, as well as enriching profession-specific knowledge and expertise.
- Continuing professional development needs to reflect current trends in practice, and adopt strategies for shared learning and multi-professional collaboration.

Action plan: benefits of collaboration, for the health and social care professions

- How can you develop/enhance your understanding of the professional implications of collaborative working? Based on the SMART criteria of setting objectives (see Introduction, pxix), devise an action plan to achieve a quality improvement in your everyday practice.

Personal/professional goal

Service/organisational goal

Thinking time: an opportunity to reflect on the professional gains of collaborative working

1 What was the criteria for entry into your professional education or training programme (qualifications, experience and personal qualities)?
   • How did you 'become' a health- and social care professional? What were the 'landmark' events in this process?
   • Has the process been focused solely within your own profession? Has any other profession shaped your professional identity?

2 Think of an example of a team with whom you have worked recently. What particular skills, attributes and values did you bring to the team?
   • Can you identify the team's shared core skills?
   • Can you identify the team's shared values and beliefs?
   • Can you identify a shared understanding and use of a team language?

3 How can this sharing of skills, knowledge and values help multi-professional collaboration?

SECTION D
PREVENTING COLLABORATION

CHAPTER **11**

Communication Restrictions

T HE PURPOSE OF THIS CHAPTER IS TO take a closer look at what can impede and ultimately derail collaboration, particularly within the arena of interpersonal communication. The focus here is on the interpersonal dynamics that are evident if a group of people work together, especially if that group is a multi-professional team. The process of interacting can be affected by the different roles individuals may play within a team, and the way they learn and make decisions together. In addition, the issue of ineffectual or overpowering leadership may also be a major factor in preventing a team moving forwards and achieving effective integrated care.

The impact of dysfunctional teamwork

Communication restrictions underpin all these manifestations of dysfunctional teamwork, which can result in fragmentation into discreet uni-professional enclaves (Hilton, 1995; White & Barriball, 1999; Coeling *et al*, 2000). Conflict is most commonly associated with communication difficulties, although this does not mean that teams literally resort to physical violence. Conflict can be expressed both verbally and non-verbally, and is more likely to be experienced as aggressively expressed views or the extreme polarisation of opinions.

It is important to note that confrontation can be part of collaborative working, and does not need to slide into the communication stalemate of conflict. Confrontation can be part of the individual's repertoire of assertive skills, as it may be necessary on occasions to be able to state and defend your particular viewpoint, which may differ from the rest of the team (Balzer Riley, 2000). Conflict, however, is a more negative communication cycle, as it can result in an impasse where misunderstanding and a lack of trust prevail, and decisions reached may be ill-considered, or fail to engage all team members whole-heartedly. Confrontation can also be viewed as a more honest and creative way of dealing with differences and diversity of opinions as opposed to more aggressive or submissive methods (Drinka *et al*, 1996).

It is only to be expected that some degree of occasional disagreement may occur within a multi-professional team. In most instances, disagreement can be a useful trigger to building cohesiveness and a positive team climate. The effective resolution of conflicting views may facilitate better team awareness, ensuring that potential misunderstandings are aired and not left to fester malignantly. If conflict is a natural experience likely to be encountered in any collaborative venture, then successful methods of conflict resolution are more crucial than trying to avoid conflict altogether. 'You know you cannot avoid conflict. What you can avoid is feeling impotent or uncomfortable when you encounter conflict situations.' (Balzer Riley, 2000).

Kinds of communication restrictions

Henneman *et al* (1995) noted that collaboration can also entail other communication difficulties, all of which may provide some sort of short-term solution, but may amplify professional differences and personal resentments in the long term (see Table 9).

At some point, all multi-professional teams may utilise a repertoire of communication methods to resolve conflict. Such methods as competition or avoidance only become problematic if used perpetually and without reflection, and if used by the same team member or professional group. To avoid getting stuck in a dysfunctional pattern of communication, Balzer Riley (2000) suggests that teams work towards a 'win-win' situation. That is, all team members are satisfied that a team decision has been discussed

99

Table 9 *The continuum of collaborative communication (adapted from Henneman et al, 1995)*

Collaboration:
- Clear and synthesised interprofessional communication focused on common purpose and a shared vision.

Cooperation:
- Clear and accessible multidisciplinary communication focused on common purpose.

Confrontation:
- Clear and accessible multidisciplinary communication focused on common purpose: one person or profession able to state openly a different view, supported by an explanation in an assertive manner.

Compromise:
- Multidisciplinary communication focused on common purpose; one person or profession moderates views or actions in an assertive manner as a method of conflict resolution.

Accommodation:
- Multidisciplinary communication focused on common purpose; one person or profession continually moderates views or actions in a submissive manner as a method of conflict resolution.

Avoidance:
- Communication lacks focus, and a common purpose is not clearly articulated; mostly uni-professional communication utilised to achieve goals and there are limited or no opportunities for multidisciplinary team meetings/consultations.

Competition:
- Communication lacks focus and a common purpose is not fully considered or apparent; mostly uni-professional communication is utilised to express covert or overt rivalries within the multidisciplinary team.

Table 9 *continued*

Conflict:
* Communication lacks focus and a common purpose, or sense of a shared vision is not apparent; uni-professional communication is utilised to express incompatibility of values or methods of working within the multidisciplinary team. Differences are not openly identified, discussed or resolved.

to the full, and a consensus arrived at fairly. With no one team member harbouring reservations or feeling excluded, a 'win-win' decision can be worth striving for, and can often produce innovative solutions.

However, there may be a number of constraints, both professional and organisational, that may restrict the 'free-falling' of unfettered problem-solving, and these need to be respected. Here the life span of the team and a sense of long-term commitment may be an advantage. Opportunities to devise 'win-win' team decisions may be more feasible in a period of stability at a later date, or after a key event where compromises had to be made in the short term.

'In their own words': an example of a lack of communication

'As an experienced Health Visitor in a new post (Primary Health Care), I arranged a series of routine hearing tests and developmental assessments for babies of eight months. This involved a parent and child attending the surgery by appointment. One mother arrived with her baby and this was the first time I had met them. I realised very quickly that the baby could not sit unsupported and was, in fact, severely disabled, and therefore this method of review was inappropriate. The parent had seen her general practitioner recently because she was concerned about the child's progress and was awaiting a paediatrician's appointment.

In my opinion, this was a failure in communication between professionals at a fundamental level, resulting in a parent being placed in a distressing position. It revealed starkly a lack of procedures and checks about passing on relevant patient information. Sufficient formalised communication channels were not in place, nor were developing informal channels sufficiently established.'

The influence of group dynamics

Communication within multi-professional teams has the added dimension of being influenced by group dynamics. Relationships within a group or team can be more multifaceted than if you are an autonomous practitioner used to dealing with clients and colleagues on a one-to-one basis. Although cohesive teams can provide a mutually supportive climate and can be an enjoyable and fruitful way of working, emotions, values, interests and styles of working can all be amplified within a group context that ultimately may inhibit or undermine effective collaboration. Burnard (1989) cites some examples of negative group dynamics, such as 'scapegoating' of one team member who gets conveniently attributed the blame for all that goes wrong. Also, assertive communication may be hampered by 'hidden agendas' – that is, individuals or professional groups having ulterior motives, which are not openly expressed, and working towards goals that are not shared by the rest of the team.

The power of group dynamics is not to be underestimated. On the one hand, a team's *esprit du corps* can buoy up an individual during difficult times and be a genuine bonus. On the other hand, negative group dynamics can result in a team member or professional sub-group feeling ostracised or undermined, with a prevailing team climate of mistrust and suspicion. Horder (1996) refers to these intricacies as the 'undertows' or the psychodynamics of interpersonal relations, stating that this is a key perspective that needs attention in successful inter-agency collaboration.

Dysfunctional group dynamics is rather like the soft underbelly of multi-professional collaboration. It is an area of collaboration that can be taken for granted ('Of course we all get on!') or is overlooked ('I'm going to get on and just do this. Involving everyone else is too much like hard work!'). Yet it can prevent the ultimate goal of collaboration, in terms of delivering integrated client-centred care. It is important here to acknowledge that it can often be difficult to be objective about a way a team works together if you are an active participant. At times, it may be difficult to put your finger exactly on what seems not to be quite right or what makes you vaguely uneasy, and rushing to blame yourself is not necessarily the answer.

In these instances, taking time to discuss and reflect on how the team communicates, is a useful skill to develop. Equally, taking the opportunity to debrief after a successful outcome or a critical 'near miss' incident, may highlight where interpersonal 'wires' get crossed and misunderstandings occur, providing a blueprint for future enhanced communication.

Roles within a multi-professional team

In addition to group dynamics, individual members may take on different roles within a team that are more congruent with preferred styles of working than any professional-specific skills or abilities. Recognising and appreciating these different roles is also a strength of collaboration, and failing to value and capitalise on a team's collective assets can also be a source of frustration and conflict. From a broad perspective, roles can be focused around getting the job done (group task) or keeping the team together (group building and maintaining) (Rungapadiachy, 1999).

Although such roles are not set in stone, it is useful to acknowledge within the team who has particular talents and a natural disposition to either keep a team on course in terms of achieving outcomes, and who is skilled at enabling and encouraging team cohesiveness. Ideally, a balance is useful as a team ruthlessly focused on meeting targets might lack the human touch, whereas too much attention to team-building may mean nothing actually gets done! Some team members may take on particular individual roles, which can contribute a useful perspective to collaborative decision-making. However, some individual roles do not readily progress the team decision-making process, and can block or sabotage consensus by negative attitudes, cynicism or opting out (Burnard, 1989).

Belbin (1993) has also devised a way of describing the different roles within a team, although the original context for these ideas stems from industry and management. Belbin categorised team roles into nine distinct types, listing personal qualities and 'allowable weaknesses'. The nine roles include the shaper (a challenging, dynamic person); the implementer (who puts ideas into action), and the resource investigator (who explores opportunities) (see Table 10). Again, these categorises are not meant to label or compartmentalise people, but rather are an acknowledgement that we cannot all do everything, and that collaboration is a blend of different professional skills and personal talents.

Using Belbin's description of team roles, it is evident that the collaborative process needs people with creative ideas ('plants'), as well

Table 10 *Team roles and characteristic phrases (from Belbin, 1993)*

1 *Plant*
Good ideas always sound strange at first.

2 *Resource investigator*
Never reinvent the wheel.

3 *Coordinator*
Has anyone else got anything to add to this?

4 *Shaper*
When the going gets tough, the tough get going.

5 *Monitor-evaluator*
This looks like the best option on balance.

6 *Teamworker*
If it's OK with you, then it's OK with me.

7 *Implementer*
Let's get down to the task in hand.

8 *Completer-finisher*
A stitch in time saves nine.

9 *Specialist*
It's better to know a lot about something than a little about everything.

as people who hold it all together as a team effort ('co-ordinator'); those who will do the work at ground level ('teamworker'), and those who will pay attention to the final details ('completers'). It is usual for team members to fulfil a number of roles, either simultaneously or for different projects. Although this may suggest a great deal of versatility, team members often have a preferred number of primary and subsidiary roles, with some team roles being positively contra-indicated or a personal anathema. For example, some team members really thrive on finishing a project properly and leaving no loose ends (a 'completer'). Other team members may not have the regard for detail, nor the patience to see a project through to the very end, and are already on to the next 'big idea' ('plant').

Knowing which team roles you have a natural affinity for is an asset, as volunteering or being allocated roles that you cannot carry out effectively can undermine self-esteem, with Belbin (1993) insisting that avoidance of unsuitable team roles should be 'actively, even energetically, pursued'.

Leadership within teams

One role within a team that causes problems with multi-professional communication is that of leader. In today's complex health- and social care organisations, healthcare professionals may have a profession-specific manager, who may be different from the day-to-day line manager, who may be different again from a project or working party manager. The notion of 'the boss', and all information and directives emanating from a single source, does not reflect current work practices. It could be asked whether a multi-professional collaborative team actually needs a leader at all, as theoretically all decisions are arrived at by consensus, implemented collectively and managed effectively.

Belbin (1993) points out that a team leader is quite a different animal from more traditional notions of a 'solo' leader. Belbin sees a team leader as a person who chooses not to do everything and delegates wisely, and is able to nurture talent within a team across the range of skills and attributes. In this respect, a team leader may take on a unique configuration of team roles, such as 'shaper' (the dynamism), 'plant' (the big idea) and 'coordinator' (refines goals and delegates tasks). A team leader may also have a preferred leadership style, and a democratic way of working may indeed suit the cooperative climate of a collaborative interpersonal team (Rungapadiachy, 1999). Other team leadership styles may be more problematic; an authoritarian leader may be too 'hands-on' and would dictate team goals and tasks, whereas a more *laissez-faire* leader would be so 'hands off' to the point of a team not being clear about its purpose or goals.

For multi-professional collaborative teams working in different health- and social care contexts, the issue of leadership is intertwined with status and the distribution of power. Within some settings, certain professions may have such weight of status, numbers and traditional hierarchies behind them that they habituate team leadership roles. As Balzer Riley (2000) points out, this can result in very different levels of perceived and actual power within a multi-professional team. Ultimately, this may have a real impact on how collaboration is embraced and achieved: 'Shifts in power are taking place in the healthcare system that will be accompanied by more opportunities for conflict resolution. The history of a power differential between nursing and medicine has made it difficult for collaboration to be used as an effective conflict management tool because collaboration rarely works well where there is wide difference in power between the groups involved'.

This acknowledgement of the varied power base of team members is essential for collaboration. The power differential within a team may generate from the perceived status of a professional group or individual (doctor versus nurse or social worker), or seniority (student versus established full-time team member). Clearly, having a team leader does serve a purpose, in terms of endeavouring to accommodate such differentials and achieving some sort of workable congruence across a multi-professional group.

Miller *et al* (1999) described 'the inspirational leader' – that is, a person with a facilitative style of leadership instrumental in 'creating and ensuring the continuation of the team culture'. An 'inspirational' team leader also uses any power with discretion and tact, and is able to accept personal limitations by delegating and using the collective talents of the team. Failing to do so may rest on a team leader's reluctance to concede an overriding controlling influence, or finding the team climate of interdependency contrary to their own professional culture or personal beliefs. Team leadership need not be a static process, but can be reviewed and rotated around team members for agreed periods and for different projects. Lone and unsupported leadership can be a fraught and stressful experience, and team leadership may operate more harmoniously if shared (co-leaders or a deputy), and if leadership skills are developed within a team as a whole.

To consider these communication restrictions in full may take a team away from the essential business in hand – namely to deliver a service, or run a department or agency. The notion that teams should and need to take time out to reflect and revise collaborative working practices can be viewed as precious time wasted. Belbin (1993) argues that a team's 'visual noise', and what seems apparent on first impressions, may not give a true picture of people's relative strengths or aptitude for certain team roles. Taking the time and opportunity to learn about each other's style of working can be beneficial to the team in the long run, and 'in reality serve to increase the prospects of success' (Belbin, 1993).

Summary of key points

- Teams will naturally experience times when not all members agree readily. Teams need to develop positive communication strategies for disclosing and resolving conflict.
- The interpersonal dynamics between team members can undermine or enhance a positive working climate.
- Team members may serve important roles within a team that are not profession-specific, but that facilitate collaboration.
- An effective team leader may offer particular qualities that can assist collaborative working.

CHAPTER 12

Service Limitations

THIS CHAPTER WILL LOOK AT the organisational issues surrounding the introduction and development of collaborative working practices. Everything may be in place for a collaborative project, such as the ideas, the personnel, the commitment and the clarity of purpose. However, these things in themselves are seldom enough without a supportive organisational infrastructure and a 'whole systems' approach to collaborative working (Barr, 1997; Calomeni *et al*, 1999).

At a day-to-day operational level, this means the management of collaboration can be a key factor in ensuring success. Ineffectual management can result in a lack of strategic vision and under-resourced, insufficiently trained multi-professional teams that can be a frustrating experience at the 'grass roots' level (Loxley, 1997). Rather like banging your head against a brick wall, multi-professional teams may experience disillusionment and mistrust of management if it is unable to convert laudable social policies and needs-led initiatives into a workable reality (Norman & Peck, 1999).

Tensions between management and collaborative teams

Perhaps at the heart of this lies practitioners' scepticism of management *per se*, and the prevailing suspicion that multi-professional collaboration is more about cost-cutting and market forces than about promoting better quality, person-centred services (Dustin, 2000; Miller *et al*, 1999). In some cases, a team may feel that it provides an already adequate service, and the amount of extra work, change, uncertainty and stress required to undertake small quality gains in service delivery is simply not worth it. Given also that management structures and personnel may change at an accelerated rate in relation to team membership, a lack of commitment to seeing changes through in the long term may create tensions between management and practitioners (Norman & Peck, 1999). In addition, practitioners may feel they were inadequately consulted about service changes, yet see themselves as being 'in the frontline' and getting 'the flak' when translating the theory into practice (Dustin, 2000).

Atkins (1998) also points out that resistance to change and a defensive attitude to anything 'new' can be the initial reaction to collaborative initiatives (see Chapter 10). The need for some enduring stability and continuity in our working lives is understandable, so innovative managerial processes and structures may face an uphill battle in motivating a reluctant and unconvinced workforce. Cherniss (1995) agrees that new roles and different ways of working require support and personal involvement in the process of change. Without this sense of 'ownership', any changes may be perceived as forced and not negotiated, resulting in greater rigidity and a lack of cooperation by the workforce.

However, a wish to conserve positive and established working practices is one thing, but obstinately burying your head in the sand without a second thought is another. Evidence at governmental, national and local levels within the UK suggests that drives for multi-professional collaboration within practice and education, and across health and social boundaries is a reality (Barr, 2000; Sweeney *et al*, 2000). It is also not just a passing whim, as authors such as Loxley (1997) map out government legislation and policy that has sought to implement effective collaboration that spans more than 30 years (since 1971). Given this impetus for collaboration, the real danger for teams is not refusal to undertake change, but how to manage changing to avoid 'policy overload' and 'role overload' (Gillam & Irvine, 2000). See Table 11.

Table 11 *Attitudes to management and managing change: proverbs and sayings*

'If it ain't broke, don't fix it.'
(It may not be perfect, but what we do at the moment does seem to work.)

'There's nothing new under the sun.'
(We've tried this before some time ago, and it didn't work then.)

'There is small choice in rotten apples.'
(None of these plans or processes are any good, they are all as bad as each other.)

'Many chimneys, but little smoke.'
(Lots being set up, but nothing really working.)

'What is new is not true, and what is true is not new.'
(Just because it's the latest trend doesn't mean to say it's any good.)

Appropriate styles of management

As Hudson (1999) notes, multi-professional collaboration cannot be forced into existing working practices. However, collaborative working may require a management approach that aims for 'cross-functional integration' across traditional disciplinary boundaries and across health- and social care (Hudson, 1999). Such an approach to management may not yet be in place, or may exist in embryonic form, but does not have the experience to fully support innovative multi-professional collaboration. This need for integrated styles of management may also be desirable for 'grey areas' of current practice, where the needs of a client group are multi-factorial and do not fit neatly into discreet health- or social care problems (Sweeney *et al*, 2000).

Miller *et al* (1999) suggest that what might be more appropriate for multi-professional collaboration is a 'directorate' style of management – namely a forum of managers drawn from across disciplines, departments or services. Here it would be important that no one professional group is

---

'In their own words': an example of collaborating across agencies

---

'An example of inter-professional collaboration is dealing with referrals for people with learning disabilities in the community: the roles and responsibilities between Social Services and the NHS Trust occupational therapists were forever unclear and under debate.

In my opinion, this was due to a lack of clear procedural guidelines, complicated by the 'grey area' of learning disabilities within the pertinent legislation governing Social Services and Occupational Therapy services. Also, there was a reluctance to accept the financial costs of interventions, in order to protect Social Services budgets. Work in some areas did lead to clarification of roles and the expertise each occupational therapist can bring. Where this has not happened, there has been a tendency towards sweeping stereotypes of 'the other team' as unwilling to take responsibility, and this was undermining the possibility of collaboration.'

over-represented or excluded, but if successful, it could provide a more integrated approach than discreet uni-professional management.

In addition, Loxley (1997) notes that the global assumption that collaboration is generally 'a good thing' prevails, and as yet there is little systematic evidence to support what is still largely wishful thinking. This can explain why it is difficult to devise any substantial managerial framework and one that addresses the often hidden costs of collaboration, such as the staff time involved in planning and coordinating projects. Barr (2000a) points out that 'a grand theory of inter-professional education is still a long way off', and this could be equally true for multi-professional practice initiatives. Any collaborative venture may take time to develop its potential, and a series of evaluative cycles may need to be completed until a clear sense of 'what works and what doesn't' emerges.

In that respect, multi-professional collaboration may be at a formative stage of describing projects and innovations in action, and it may yet be too soon to draw any firm conclusions or devise a 'grand theory'. The danger here is that management practices may move on to the next 'big thing,' or the next wave of social policy directives, or the next wave of reorganisation, without allowing sufficient time and opportunity for viable and effective projects to flourish. 'For it is the frontline professionals and related staff who will have to deliver integrated care to service users, and, if their relationships are not clear and constructive, then broad inter-agency strategies may fail' (Hudson, 1999).

Accounting for differences

Managing multi-professional collaboration presents a range of challenges that require skilful handling both at the service level (strategic) and also at the 'coalface' (daily practice). Hudson (1999) describes a number of barriers to collaboration, including an acknowledgement that teams may have multi-professional differences (see Table 12).

Often the most pervasive of these is recognising that different models of care shape the way professional groups think and act (Meads & Ashcroft, 2000; Sweeney *et al*, 2000). There could be conflict or misunderstanding in a team if some professions adhere to a social model of care (focus on societal explanations of health and ill health) versus adherence to a more medical model (focus on bio-physiological causes of illness). As these contrasting models may be an integral part of pre-registration education and professional socialisation, the subsequent values and approach to healthcare are often deeply ingrained (Peck & Norman, 1999). A merger of models can produce a shared 'bio-psycho-social model' which embraces a more holistic view of health and healthcare. However, a dichotomy of views can have an impact across the spectrum of collaboration, in terms of comprehensively assessing a client's needs and agreeing team goals (Sweeney *et al*, 2000).

Integrating and managing such a variety of values, philosophies, skills and roles may appear to be an almost insurmountable task. Also, the pressure is on to deliver, as opposed to being able to simply mouth the rhetoric of collaboration. As Barr (1997) points out, real progress is measured in terms of outcomes and improved service delivery: 'There is no room for teams that are teams in name only and would more accurately be described as fragmented groups. An interdisciplinary team is only worth having if it is effective in achieving agreed aims and goals that lead to a more focused, responsive and individualised service for clients and their families.'

Table 12 *The management of collaborative teams (based on Hudson, 1999)*

- Multi-professional teams may have different patterns of employment (hours, duration of contracts, terms and conditions).

- Multi-professional teams may have different lines of accountability (line manager, professional head).

- Multi-professional teams may have different ways of making decisions (protocol and procedures, custom and practice).

- Multi-professional teams may have different perceptions of the benefits and drawbacks of collaboration (cost-effectiveness and time-efficiency, short-term versus long-term gains).

- Multi-professional teams may have different values concerning health and maintaining health (social versus medical model, the 'art' versus the science of practice).

Although not aimed specifically at the management of multi-professional collaboration, Loxley (1997) does recommend some core processes that can facilitate the development of projects. These include a shared approach to assessment, or 'naming and framing' the remit of the team by utilising agreed common terminology and concepts. Management processes could entail the effective and equitable use of resources across a team, and ensuring that structures are in place that allow for a cross-fertilisation of information and ideas. This does not mean swamping a team with a flurry of meetings or ruthlessly rationing stationery per capita, but the designing of sensible, measured working practices.

Such ways of working need to be agreed, planned, put into action and targeted at different levels of intervention 'so that it moves multi-professional collaboration from the realm of enthusiast's hope to a practical proposition' (Loxley, 1997). To this effect, adapting existing structures and processes may be a better way to manage progress than 're-inventing the wheel'. Over time 'gaps' in service provision and lines of communication may emerge and may need to be resolved. However, managing collaboration with a brand new infrastructure makes it difficult to phase in changes or to evaluate progress without an established baseline.

Collaboration and management cultures

For multi-professional collaboration to develop and succeed, it needs to be a recognised, resourced and formal activity (Loxley, 1997). If left to the inspired few, it can be in danger of fading out once the first wave of enthusiasm subsides or the particular acolytes leave. It needs to become an active and mainstream part of the management culture if it is to overcome the many practical and ideological problems that may not allow it to even get out of the starting gate, let alone win the race of achieving quality service improvements (Riley, 1997). Meads and Ashcroft (2000) also differentiate between 'quick-fix' training versus real education, which aims to 'reinforce the common ground from which the opportunities for collaboration will grow.

It is worth noting that multi-professional teams may not have the time, skills or confidence to initiate team-building activities for themselves. This is where supportive management can identify and address learning needs and provide tailored opportunities, using external resources and facilitators where appropriate. Although the amount of time this entails may seem a deterrent initially, there is some evidence to suggest the long-term gains of developing a skilled team include more efficient communications and enhanced joint working (Lewis *et al*, 1998).

A reassuring end point is to acknowledge that multi-professional collaboration is not a corporate, faceless juggernaut, but is the collective endeavour of a group of individuals with different skills, professions and backgrounds. Loxley (1997) states that the attitude of team members and their willingness to learn from each other is an important factor in establishing a climate for change. This 'mind-set' may already be present in existing groups of professionals, but needs enabling and empowering management to spot it and nurture it. 'The real payoff in working with others comes when you gain more from the collaboration than is necessary because of your interdependency, when you gain more from joining forces than together you put in, when the whole is greater than the sum of the parts, when there is synergy' (Iles, 1997). (See Table 13.)

Table 13 *Management strategies for supporting collaboration (from Barr, 1997; Forman, 1998; Loxley, 1997; Sweeney et al, 2000)*

- Inclusive strategic planning
- Operational procedures review (clear protocols)
- Inter-professional clinical audits (common standards)
- Joint assessment procedures and protocol
- Collaborative care pathways
- Joint service provision ('one-stop shop')
- Joint commissioning and funding of services (across agencies)
- Joint training programmes, 'away days' and work-based learning
- Joint induction programmes
- Inter-professional mentoring and supervision
- Continuing professional development (CPD)
- Significant event auditing (forum for reviewing practice issues and initiatives)
- Evidence-based workshops (critical appraisal skills)

Summary of key points

- Tensions may exist between practitioners and management that may reflect on how new initiatives are received and implemented. These tensions need to be addressed to ensure effective multi-professional collaboration.
- Multi-professional collaboration may require more 'cross-functional' and integrated styles of management.
- Managers need to recognise and account for professional differences within multi-professional teams and services.
- Multi-professional collaboration needs to become a mainstream management activity, supported by such initiatives as team-building, joint training programmes and an inclusive approach to strategic planning.

CHAPTER 13

Professional Barriers

IN THE PREVIOUS SECTION, THE BENEFITS OF multi-professional collaboration were explored. Realistically, the possible barriers to collaboration need to be fully considered before getting carried away with an innovative idea to transform multi-professional practice. The previous two chapters have detailed barriers such as poor team communication and ineffective management.

However, some of the barriers to collaboration can be laid squarely on our own doorstep and are to do with us, as professionals and as people. This chapter details the professional barriers that undeniably exert an influence on collaboration, such as passive assumptions and stereotyping, role boundaries and tribalism. There have been many misconceptions of role function cited in the literature that have prevented successful collaborative practice. The lack of common goals and a commitment to collaboration, or a lack of mutual trust and respect, can have a disastrous effect on the team's ability to collaborate effectively (see Chapter 14). Ineffective interpersonal communication or professional insecurity can also erode the individual's ability to be collaborative and work within a multi-professional context (Lichtenstein *et al*, 1997). No one ever claimed that multi-professional collaboration was going to be easy, but with insight and diligence, obstacles to collaboration need not become crash barriers, and can be circumnavigated or avoided altogether.

Role assumptions and professional stereotyping

Negative stereotypes with respect to professional images are prevalent in society, despite the fact that we may feel we are living in more 'enlightened' times. Professional images that are nothing more than unhelpful caricatures abound in the media, and in popular gossip and myth. When such stereotypes go unchallenged, and ossify into passive assumptions masquerading as 'fact', it can be difficult to accept a health- and social care professional as they really are.

A stereotype may be defined as a person or thing that conforms to an unjustifiably fixed, standardised mental picture. Stereotypes are often formed through the process of socialisation, where exposure to others influences how people learn to function within a culture (Christman, 1991). Socialisation offers insight into how culture affects the roles professionals enact and the expectations they have of others. This process is mediated through limited personal experiences that can lead to generalisations, the historical legacy of a profession and, probably most importantly, media portrayal of a profession (see Chapter 10).

An example of a classic stereotype widely referred to in the UK popular press and media is that of nurses as 'angels', 'battle-axe matrons', or doctor's 'handmaidens' (O'Dowd, 1998). Even though these represent stereotypes rather than reality, other professions may make judgements about a professional role without an understanding of the culture, history or philosophical stance of that particular profession. Taking the above example further, it would explain attitudinal problems in the workplace, such as a doctor's expectation that nursing is subservient to the established and legitimatised culture of the medical profession (Walby *et al*, 1994). Historically, the nurse's role was to carry out orders rather than to be an independent decision-maker (Duffield & Lumby, 1994).

As a result of this cultural context, nurses have tried to influence clinical decisions using subtle strategies such as the 'doctor-nurse game', as described by Stein (1967). Nurses phrased clinical opinions in such a way as to make it appear that they were initiated by the doctor. The evolution of professional roles in the changing context of health- and social care make out-dated stereotypes redundant. Alarmingly, even glib asides and misguided 'jokes' can pollute a team climate and obstruct a willingness to work collaboratively. Today's health- and social care professionals need to utilise more effective communication channels that do not rely on subterfuge, manipulation or negative psychology. With a more universal acceptance of a multi-professional approach to clinical reasoning and decision-making, a client-centred approach to care can serve as the predominant focus of the healthcare team.

Changing passive assumptions

As health- and social care professionals, we all need to take an active responsibility for our profession's identity and perceived public image. We need to play our part by not reinforcing the negative stereotypes we have inherited, and by being more confident in asserting our current skills and abilities (see Chapters 15 and 16). For example, there is a demand for nurses to develop their confidence and assertiveness in the multidisciplinary arena, and to value their own knowledge, especially if they expect others to value it too (Busby & Gilchrist, 1992).

This relies on practitioners utilising their knowledge of the client and the clinical context to inform decision-making. This in itself has implications for the development of professional roles, taking practitioners into non-traditional, and unique, health- and social care settings. Indeed, 'knowing the client' was cited by nurses as a crucial factor that boosted nurses' sense of professionalism and confidence to advocate actively for the client, thereby contributing to multi-disciplinary decision-making (Lovelady, 1998). When the nurse did not know the client, the reverse was observed; even when invited to contribute to the discussion, the nurse was unable to contribute in such a meaningful way. This example has relevance for all health- and social care professionals, in terms of being confident and able to articulate your professional role. Also, this needs to be grounded in the realities of practice and not based on guesswork or hopeful aspirations.

All professionals need to build on their strengths in order to make a positive contribution to the delivery of client-centred care. As roles develop and boundaries shift, all professions needs to acknowledge the increased accountability for their professional decisions and the consequences of their actions, without this becoming a barrier to ground-breaking and innovative role progression. 'The reason that blurring, converging, fusing or collapsing role boundaries are perceived as problematic is that they change and might threaten professional rights and responsibilities. This becomes even more difficult when the change or threat is indeterminate, and is not addressed explicitly. When one's role is not clear, it is not possible to be sure that one is fulfilling one's obligations, or that one has been accused unjustly of not fulfilling one's obligations' (Dombeck, 1997).

The evolving health and social care professions

The design and delivery of health- and social care is undeniably evolving at a rapid rate. In terms of professional roles, there is the recent initiative in the UK of nurse consultant and therapist consultant posts, with the promise of consultant posts for other health- and social care professions.

In terms of delivery, there are a myriad health- and social care services run by professions other than medicine. However, although the structure is changing rapidly, it is difficult to change the prevailing professional or workplace culture at the same pace. Professional socialisation may be partly responsible for fostering attitudes to other professions, determining values that shape attitudes to other members of the multi-professional team (see Chapter 16).

Reflecting on my teaching experiences to date, it is evident that even first-year undergraduate students are willing to address the nature of attitude formation and its impact on professional identities. Here it is essential not to assume that students are 'clean slates', but rather to acknowledge the existence of both positive and negative assumptions of different professions, due to their interaction with society and their own life experiences. Opportunities to identify and address differing perceptions of professional groups can generate much discussion, which in itself can be a valid learning outcome. However, this can be accompanied by a sense of unease if it is felt that debating such issues has, in fact, reinforced previously held stereotypes and not dispelled them. Appreciating how professional identities form over time may require us to take a more long-term view of recognising and challenging commonly held unproductive assumptions. There is, perhaps, a distinction between opportunities to discuss versus informed and skilfully facilitated multi-professional debate.

However, positive assumptions can be a constructive and pro-active way of organising and learning from experiences, whereas negative assumptions may impede a student's learning from a multi-professional context. The rationale here is that undergraduate inter-professional education provides students with opportunities to recognise and relinquish unhelpful and unfounded professional stereotypes at a formative stage of the education process (Barr, 1998). Dombeck (1997) proposes that 'a step-wise process of cultural sensitization' between disciplines is necessary in order to successfully encourage a multi-professional perspective on collaboration, which could be pursued with equal vigour at pre-registration and post-qualifying stages.

Tribalism and uni-professional 'territories'

As health- and social care professional roles have been gradually expanding over the last decade, there has been a cautionary note across the literature not to lose sight of the purpose of these developments. As professionals strive to define and extend the boundaries of their role, possibly against some resistance, it might be easy to lose the client-centred focus in the politics of ring-fencing profession-specific 'territories'. If this occurs, then professionals run the risk of tribalism and operating like a 'tribe' to protect their own professional 'patch'. Here the focus can change from being client-centred, to exercising professional control in order to enhance status and ensure exclusive possession of particular clinical skills.

The drive for clinical leadership within each of the health- and social care professions is important for raising standards and developing practice. However, it needs to be acknowledged that for some particularly complex clients, and in particular clinical or rehabilitation settings, a multi-disciplinary approach will always be necessary. It is crucial to recognise that each profession has its contribution to make, and it can be inappropriate to start battling over who does what. The message therefore is that impartial professional judgement should determine which approach is best for the client and for the clinical context. Indeed, new roles may accentuate the need for teamworking and valuing each profession's unique contribution, rather than allowing one professional group to dominate with the others unheard or not consulted.

It is hoped that truly valuing team collaboration will increase the chances of gaining consensus. There is evidence that even if the decision then does not follow an individual practitioner's preference, if their contribution has been acknowledged and they understand the rationale for the final decision, then it is more likely to be accepted. As a team decision, this is more likely to be supported by all members and results in consistency and continuity of care.

Practical ways of removing barriers to collaboration

There are many examples of successful collaboration where the fundamentals of trust, mutual respect and effective teamwork have prevailed. Health- and social care professions need more exposure to each other outside the specific clinical arena in order to understand each other's perspectives in a fresh context. Multidisciplinary education and audit should be encouraged at all levels (Baggs, 1994), and any dialogue that promotes understanding of the philosophical tenets of each profession is to be valued. Case-study review or joint audit gives professions an opportunity to explore the outcome of their decision-making for clients, and hopefully inform future practice. By developing a core of common team experiences and interpreting them in the light of shared professional accountability, this might lead to more open discussion and reflection of sensitive practice issues.

Barriers to collaboration may not be just what we do and say as health- and social care professionals, but what we wear. Richardson (1999) cites uniforms as reinforcing professional stereotypes, but acknowledges that this has positive and negative aspects. For example, nurses uniforms may help to identify staff and act as a symbol of competence and professionalism, but can also reflect hierarchical expectations and delineate a social distance. Unless professionals are mindful of these potential barriers to communication, their ability to forge successful collaborative relationships may be hindered.

Another common barrier to collaboration in practice is the alienating effect of language. Indeed, this is so fundamental that we have discussed the divisive nature of exclusive professional language from a range of perspectives throughout this book (see Chapters 15 and 16). Clients need to be given information in a way that they can readily understand and see the direct relevance for their particular circumstances. This also extends to interdisciplinary discussions, where abbreviations both written and verbal are not helpful unless they are clearly understood by the whole team. It is difficult to communicate, let alone collaborate, when team members are not speaking on the same terms.

Abbreviations abound and are inevitable in the health and care sector, and can become a kind of workplace 'shorthand'. However, the frequent use of abbreviations and profession-specific terms can also sound like an indecipherable code to the novice team member or a newly-referred client. This hurdle can be overcome by being aware of this, creating an environment where people can easily seek clarification, without judgement and by more shared multi-professional dialogue in journals, conferences and education.

Putting aside professional egos and historical grudges

It can be seen that there are many potential barriers to collaboration, both within and across professions, that need to be overcome. Multi-professional education across all professions and more collaborative activities have been cited as ways to counter the passive assumptions we may have developed through our own experiences, socialisation and exposure to media influences. The hope is that by recognising the stereotypes we hold, negative assumptions can be transformed into a willingness to learn. It is important, as new roles develop across professions and the boundaries of practice are redrawn, that client-centred care is not subsumed by tribalism and political battles to assert authority. Learning to collaborate is about putting aside professional egos and historical grudges, in order to get on with the job of providing quality services.

Summary of key points

- Passive assumptions about other professional groups can lead to unhelpful and confining stereotyping.
- Roles and responsibilities of the healthcare professions are evolving, placing more emphasis on the need to be more assertive in articulating a relevant and contemporary professional identity.
- Multi-professional education at pre-registration may have a part to play in countering the negative effects of professional stereotyping, but this needs to be reviewed critically in terms of who is included and when it occurs.
- There are a number of barriers to collaboration, although clear and commonly shared language between professional groups is crucial if these barriers are to be overcome.

SECTION E

DEMONSTRATING COLLABORATION

CHAPTER 14

The Fundamentals: Mutual Trust and Respect

OF ALL THE PERSONAL ATTRIBUTES AND key characteristics cited as being necessary for effective collaboration, trust and respect seem to be the most pervasive. Indeed, it is not uncommon to find these two characteristics bound inseparably to each other, almost expressed as a single notion, as if they are mutually inclusive (Henneman *et al*, 1995; Papadopoulos *et al*, 1998; Purtilo & Haddad, 1996). Evident in the way that both trust or respect are described, is the view that a fundamental dynamic of collaborative working is about relating to another person (Purtilo & Haddad, 1996). Both trust and respect are not the requirements for how one person should behave to another, but describe a climate of cooperation. This needs to be established and maintained if a client is to work with a healthcare professional, or if members of a multi-disciplinary team are to work together effectively.

Starting with realistic expectations

Establishing mutual trust and respect with a newly referred client or within a team is not just a preliminary stage in collaborative partnership that you can simply tick off from a checklist of requirements. It is more a state of perpetual readiness, which a practitioner can actively demonstrate through professional attitudes and skills. This is essentially about being reliable and consistent in your approach to clients and colleagues, and people having confidence that you are open and fair-minded. Setting up this climate of trust and respect is sometimes described as establishing 'rapport' (Cooley, 2000; Masin, in Davis, 1998; Williams, 1997), enhanced by such relationship attitudes as being a warm, empathetic and open communicator (Cooley, 2000; Heron 1990; Rungapadiachy, 1999).

Figure 7 A climate of trust and respect: establishing rapport

As a novice practitioner, you can often feel overwhelmed by all the laudable characteristics you are meant to demonstrate in all encounters with all clients and colleagues at all times. Although hard to dispute the calibre of 'unconditional positive regard' (Parton, 1998; Rogers, 1980; Minardi & Riley, 1997) or 'congruence' as positive aspects in a therapeutic relationship, it can often set up impossibly high expectations that you will always say and do 'the right thing'. Heron (1990) aptly reminds us that interpersonal skills are chiefly about being human and expressing that humanity, in all its idiosyncratic ways and within a vast number of different encounters. Stating that these human skills are 'macculate', and therefore no one is perfect all the time, can be a way of putting personal and professional requirements for successful collaboration into a realistic, achievable context.

Although it can be instructive to be aware of ideal standards for positive and empowering interpersonal communication, perhaps it is just as useful to explore what happens when trust and respect are not present or are not mutual. Also, it could be argued that being trustworthy and respectful are to do with utilising the more specialist skills of counselling over an evolving professional relationship and have no real place in routine, transient healthcare encounters. But striking up an immediate understanding with another person or persons has its value regardless of timescales or intended treatment goals. As stated by Rungapadiachy (1999), 'trust is the foundation of all interpersonal relationships', thus trust and respect underlie all professional health- and social care interactions.

Trusting and being trustworthy

One reason why trust is so fundamental to collaborative partnerships is that you can trace its origins in human social development back to early infancy. As theorised by Erikson (1963), human psychosocial development evolves over eight key stages from birth to adulthood. The first stage, from birth to 12 months, is epitomised by the theme of trust versus mistrust, manifested in the bonding relationship a child has with its mother or principal carer. During this stage, an infant is absolutely dependent upon another person for its basic needs to survive and thrive (Bee, 1994). In this state of dependency, a child can feel vulnerable, anxious and in need of reassurance that it will not be abandoned or forgotten. Here the carer's ability to be consistent, predictable and reliable are important features of the infant learning that it can trust and depend on another person. A child's early experiences of mistrust, abandonment and neglect can all have profound repercussions on the formation and maintenance of intimate relationships in adult life (Davis, 1998).

The very antithesis of the trusting relationship is when confidences are broken, friendships betrayed and partnerships damaged through deceit and ulterior motives. With little additional assistance from the imagination, mistrust sets the scene for powerful emotive themes often explored to full effect in the arts and the media. Examples of wronged lovers, partners of friends blurting out 'But I trusted you!' are all too often the climax of a television soap opera episode, novel or play. Indeed, embedded in our own personal histories are occasions when we too have been let down or disappointed by someone we trusted, and whom we thought was deserving of that trust. Although it is apparent that professional collaboration is not a stage for such outpourings of high drama, we can still remain wary and circumspect of colleagues until that initial trusting connection has been established.

But what does it really mean to be 'trustworthy'? It sounds as if to be worthy of trust involves some kind of colossal struggle, or is the final reward for a gruelling endeavour – all sweat and sacrifice. However, McLeod (1998) offers the notion of 'personal soundness' as desirable qualities for a therapist. In terms of professional collaboration, personal soundness translates as someone whose dealings with colleagues are untainted by personal agendas or unfounded misconceptions. Heron (1990) talks of the helping relationship being built on the 'emotional competence' of the helper, again suggesting a sense of safety and robustness. Heron (1990) also describes a helper demonstrating a 'helping grace', characterised by such attributes as a warm concern for others, openness and an authentic presence. More recently, the NHS Plan (Department of Health, 2000c) coined the phrase 'principled motivation' to describe the dedication of the NHS staff to delivering a service to the public 'glued together by a bond of trust'.

Although these notions are essentially describing the client-centred therapist relationship, the same elements of soundness, competence and authenticity ring equally true for collaborative relationships with colleagues. Perhaps Rogers (1980) best sums up the elusiveness of trust

Table 14 *A trusting person is… (from Sundeen et al, 1998)*

- Self-aware
- Able to share self-awareness with others
- Accepting of others
- Open to new experiences
- Capable of maintaining long-term consistency between words and action
- Able to delay or transcend their own needs

and being trustworthy as a fundamental belief and an 'essential confidence in the capacity of the human organism' (see Table 14). Hence trust is built on the belief that a colleague has the capacity of potential to work collaboratively in a constructive manner, and that an initial trusting connection can be deepened and enriched by time, effort and productive outcomes.

'In their own words': trusting and respecting

Inter-professional collaboration is about 'trusting and respecting each other as professionals. It is also about respecting the diversity of approaches which are needed to enable clients to achieve their goals.'

Respecting diversity and tolerating differences

What, then, of respect? At first glance, respect seems to convey a feudal or hierarchical relationship – the lord of the manor expects respect from the serfs on his land, and the older generation feels entitled to respect from the younger generation. Inherent in this equation is a sense of deference, of one person conceding to another in terms of power, age, money or status. This is perhaps unfortunate, as respect within professional collaboration is more to do with respecting differences and tolerating other points of view: it is a meeting of equals and the creation of a relationship built on cooperation, not domination.

Demonstrating respect entails appreciating the diversity of other people's backgrounds and how this is reflected in the way people think, feel and act (see Chapter 6). Professional collaboration can mean accounting for other colleagues' personal and professional histories, as well as respecting a colleague's views in terms of age, gender and culture. Bland indifference or reluctant, begrudging acknowledgement, is not the same as valuing the many different ways colleagues may frame and interpret a problem or propose a clinical intervention. Occasionally, this may seem like hard work, or unnecessarily complicated when you have speedily arrived at a particular solution by your own route, and the dogma of 'political correctness' seems artificially nit-picking and impractical.

However, taking the time to note and value diversity is part and parcel of today's world (Kreps & Kinimoto, 1994). Although the notion of cultural diversity and culturally sensitive practice is well established, the transcultural skills of being trustworthy and accepting are just as valid within healthcare teams as they are with clients (Papadopoulos *et al*, 1998).

Purtilo and Haddad (1996) described respect within a client-professional relationship as a mutual constructive dependence. Within professional collaborative relationships, this can be translated as a positive reliance on each team member's knowledge, skills and judgement, in order to arrive at the most workable clinical decision or service initiative.

'In their own words': but the obvious doesn't always happen

Some people welcome you with open arms initially but support doesn't necessarily follow, others may be more cautious and you may need to earn their trust. Once you have earned their trust, surprising things can happen. I have found it important to avoid getting into status games and always put the client's needs first. Sounds obvious, but the obvious doesn't always happen.'

Being respectful and tolerating differences is put to the test most when dealing with emergencies and with unique situations that have no precedence or formulaic response. Here it can be all too easy to focus on differences as an excuse to attribute blame or to vent anger, and for a team to fragment into resentments. Clearly, for respect to be 'a deep and genuine presence' (Hawtin & Moore, 1998) it needs to be steadfast and durable. As this echoes the qualities of soundness and competence, it is perhaps understandable to see why trust and respect are so often intertwined; they both require consistent, sustained effort in order to endure.

Trust and respect as dynamic processes

The core of the interplay between trust and respect is that it is a dynamic, evolving process between two or more equal partners. The notion of 'mutuality' or reciprocity is well accepted within the context of the client-therapist relationship (Masin, in Davis, 1998; Mitchell, 1995; Peloquin, 1989; Purtilo & Haddad, 1996; Rungapadiachy, 1999). However, mutuality is also a key component of professional collaboration. This does not mean that you keep score of the favours you are owed or carefully weigh up each contribution you make to collective team decisions. Creative and fruitful collaboration is built more on the sense of a positive alliance, drawing on each other's professional skills and personal qualities at different times for different tasks over different timescales. No one keeps a tally, no one feels under- or over-utilised, no one shoulders all the responsibility all the time, and all team members feel able to receive help or support as well as to give.

You may feel that this brings us full circle to expecting impossibly high standards for collaborative practice, and these fundamentals of mutual trust and respect are unrealistic in the context of a busy department or under-resourced service. However, these 'fundamentals' of collaboration ensure that a safe and secure working environment is established, and can form the basis of effective teamwork in the short and long term. Safety and a sense of stability are a fundamental human need and proved a context for us to value what is familiar, as well as nurturing the confidence to take risks and explore the unfamiliar (Maslow, 1987; Minardi & Riley, 1997) (see Chapter 6).

Building up a climate of mutual trust and respect makes it easier for a collaborative team to respond positively to change, meet challenges creatively and be sensitive to the ebb and flow of team membership. For these reasons, trust and respect within teams may be built up in stages or propelled forward by key events, best conceptualised as a wave or spiral of evolution (Mitchell, 1995; Rungapadiachy, 1999). It is also evident that in the development of collaborative working, actions have to match promises and there needs to be a consistency between word and deed. Blind trust and sycophantic respect can be just as unhelpful as no trust or respect at all (Purtilo & Haddad, 1996).

If the development of the fundamentals of collaboration is never-ending and more cyclical than linear, how do you know when your team has reached a reasonable state of mutual trust and respect? The answer probably lies in a scrutiny of your team's working practices, such as how decisions are made; how meetings are conducted; how the team receives and shapes new ideas or implements social policy directives. It can also be characterised in a working atmosphere that has energy and direction, where team members feel equally free to take on new ideas and more tasks as well as being able to define limits and say 'no'. In short, the business of collaborative practice is conducted with a regard for the individual.

Summary of key points
- Trust and respect are fundamental to effective collaborative practice, setting up a 'climate of cooperation'.
- Trusting a colleague and being trustworthy can be described as the ability to be consistent, sound and authentic.
- Respect is an ability to accept and tolerate differences, whether professional, personal or social.
- Trust and respect are not one-sided, one-off interactions, but require a sense of mutual giving and receiving within a team in order to flourish.

Action plan: demonstrating collaboration – the fundamentals

- How can you develop/enhance your understanding of mutual trust and respect? Based on the SMART criteria for setting objectives (see Introduction, pxix) devise an action plan to achieve a quality improvement in your everyday practice.

Personal/professional goal

Service/organisational goal

Thinking time: an opportunity to reflect on the fundamentals of collaboration

1 Reflect back over positive events that have happened to you at school, at work, and when pursuing a particular hobby or sport. When and who did you trust, and in what circumstances?

2 How did this trusted person demonstrate soundness, consistency and authenticity (in words and actions)?
   - At school
   - In team games or a sport
   - At a social event
   - Starting a new job or joining a new club
   - Undertaking a period of study or training and learning a new skill.

   Think about how this feeling of containment and safety can be applied to collaborative working. Can you illustrate this with an example of a crisis or challenge and how it was managed?

3 Masin suggests that you can pose three questions to avoid bias and come to a better understanding of diversity (in Davis, 1998). Select some key workplace practices, such as referral protocols, convening and holding meetings, communication networks and the induction of new team members, and consider the contribution of each team member.
   - How is this colleague like all human beings?
   - How is this colleague like some human beings?
   - How is this colleague like no other human being?

CHAPTER 15

The Essentials: Interpersonal Communication

A T THE HEART OF COLLABORATION is effective communication – the ability of members of the healthcare team to interact with one another and, just as importantly, with clients, carers and other external agencies. This kind of communication between individuals and within groups is called interpersonal communication, and it takes many forms. The ones we shall be discussing here are: attending and listening; giving and receiving feedback; assertiveness, and handling and resolving conflict.

In earlier chapters, we considered barriers to communication, and many of these barriers can be attributed to limitations in the skills of interpersonal communication (see Chapter 11). One of the essential skills in collaboration is the demonstration of interest in and attending to what others are communicating, both verbally and non-verbally.

This sounds so simple one would assume that we attend to others all of the time. However, as we are constantly bombarded by sensory information from a variety of sources, it is inevitable that we attend only to a small percentage of information at any one time.

Attending and active listening as essential skills
Our sensory organs are continually picking up messages from external input in the form of sounds, visual images, smells and changes in temperature,

while at the same time our internal sensory systems are relaying messages related to stress, fatigue, pain, anxiety or hunger. It is impossible to pay attention to every message simultaneously, and we would overload our sensory systems if we attempted to do so. Therefore, we tend to pay attention to what we perceive as important at that point in time. This decision may be based on our value system and what we rank as important – the work situation, a problem at home, or a searing headache.

While it is reasonable to excuse people from attending fully to what we are saying, if we are aware they have another urgent or pressing consideration, all too often this is not the case. In day-to-day communication people either do not attend to others, or give the appearance of not attending, either deliberately or unintentionally. Clearly, as healthcare professionals, we need to be aware of our level of attending and to avoid being considered by clients or colleagues as unconcerned or uninterested. So, how can we positively demonstrate that we are attending to others?

In selecting what we attend to, we are basing our decision on what we see as important and what we value. This assumes that our values are the correct ones and this is, of course, based entirely on our own judgement. If we pay attention to others we are overtly demonstrating that we value their contribution. This does not mean we necessarily agree with what they are saying, but we are recognising its worth. In doing so not only does the giver of information feel valued but, in turn, by keeping an open mind, new information can be gained or perceptions challenged. Therefore, giving attention to others is partly about making a conscious decision to concentrate on, and open your mind to, other views and to consider them without bias.

Attention is most potently demonstrated by the use of appropriate body language. This includes eye contact, and non-verbal positive feedback, such as nods and sympathetic expressions, and this can demonstrate that the speaker is offering a valid and valued opinion. As you become more skilled at paying attention, you will become practised at looking behind the verbal message and interpreting the non-verbal messages. This is termed looking for the congruency in an interaction. A communication is termed congruent when the verbal and non-verbal messages are mutually reinforcing. Lack of congruency points towards a mismatch in what the words say and how the speaker feels, and highlights the need for further clarification or restating the intended message more clearly.

Just how powerful the act of attending is within interpersonal communication is exemplified by Gage (1998): 'It did not matter whether the participant was a health professional or a client, the issue of feeling heard was raised with considerable emotion. It would appear that attending to the need to feel heard is critical to the establishment of a synergic relationship.'

Potential decoding errors and enhancing message accuracy

Attention then is the precursor to active listening – an essential stage in effective interpersonal communications. In the context of busy lives and demanding work schedules, honest and sustained active listening can be difficult to put into action. How often do we feel like saying to people 'You are listening, but you do not hear what I am saying!' Absorbing the words and understanding the meaning are not necessarily the same things. One of the ways in which communication can break down is a so-called decoding error, when the relayed message is received, but the meaning is misinterpreted.

One of the reasons that this occurs is because we all use different codes for interpreting information. These codes can be similar but they can vary greatly. In the healthcare setting it is surprising how many different professional 'languages' exist. These languages may be organisation- or discipline-related. Drawing on a local example, a qualified healthcare professional who supervises students on clinical placement can be referred to as a mentor (nursing-specific term), a clinical educator (physiotherapy-specific term), or a fieldwork educator (occupational therapy-specific term). If we, as healthcare professionals, struggle with discipline-specific terminology, how much more difficult is it for clients or carers, or if the language used is not the first language of the recipient?

Decoding is not just about language, it is also based on the background, culture and values of both the sender and receiver. If someone buys a dress and tells you it was expensive or 'cost the earth', you may hazard a guess at the possible price. How accurate your estimate will be will depend on the similarity of your lifestyle, income and importance of clothes to you both. If the sender and receiver do not appreciate these potential variables, there is the likelihood of the message being decoded inaccurately, creating a chink or a chasm of misunderstanding.

In healthcare these potential decoder errors can be much more crucial, and often occur when a client relays subjective information relating to pain, anxiety, distress, intimate relationships and personal feelings. A client may say the pain 'is not too bad, thanks', so nothing is offered for pain relief, whereas that particular client may have been understating the pain as their cultural background may discourage overt expressions of emotions. A healthcare practitioner sensitised to the multiple meanings behind one subjective statement needs to seek clarification in order to identify the concealed message, offering pain relief as a possible option.

In order to accurately decipher the correct message we need to be aware of the potential for decoding errors. How then can we be sure that we have received accurate information? One method is that of reflecting back the key points to the sender. This is not about repeating back word for word what the sender has said, but is a skilful method of summarising the main message, so that the sender can confirm that you have both accurately heard the words, acknowledged the facts and interpreted the meaning.

Giving and receiving feedback to promote a 'team spirit'

In collaborative working, it is vital for members of the team, including the client, to be willing to offer information or opinions, in order to maximise the team potential and for decisions to be made and put into action. If effective interpersonal communication is to occur, time must be set aside for the sharing of information and the receiving of feedback. Collaborative teamwork will only thrive when team members are encouraged to voice their opinions openly and to give feedback without fear of retribution (Gage 1998).

Feedback is an important component of interpersonal communication. It can be both verbal ('that's a good idea') and non-verbal (nodding your head in agreement), and team members will be encouraged to offer further information and specific observations if they receive positive cues from the members of the group. All of us like to receive positive feedback and teamwork is enhanced when good ideas and opinions are acknowledged and received with at least a modicum of enthusiasm. Realistically, not all feedback can always be positive, and alternative views or constructive criticism may be necessary. If negative feedback is to be given it is important to consider how best to approach the situation without totally extinguishing all flickers of initiative. Even oblique observations and obscure information may have their time and place.

If one individual has been singled out for criticism, it may be appropriate for that to be discussed in a small group or on a one-to-one basis. The main points need to be made calmly and in a non-aggressive manner, using concrete examples wherever possible. Remember, giving negative feedback is still a two-way process, and the person receiving criticism must have the opportunity to respond. If the whole team is discussing a particularly sensitive issue and negative comments are being made, these should be balanced with positive feedback where possible. All discussion items need to be reviewed objectively, without reference to personal agendas or individual personalities.

These genuine and adult exchanges of views can engender a feeling of a 'team spirit', which can enhance multi-professional collaboration. When team spirit exists, all members of the team are willing to share information and professional rivalries can dissipate. As everyone's input is valued, information can be shared, understood and disseminated co-operatively. 'Team spirit exists when all participants believe that they belong to the team and that they can openly request and give feedback without fear of retribution' (Gage, 1998).

Assertiveness as an essential skill for collaboration

In the discussion concerning giving feedback, it was identified that this can require sensitivity, particularly when feedback is negative. It can also be very difficult receiving negative feedback, even if it is felt to be justified. One of the key skills often mentioned to assist with situations like this is the skill of being assertive. Although this is a high-profile skill in many business and self-help domains, considering assertiveness within the context of multi-professional collaboration is a timely reminder that difficult situations do arise and need skilful handling.

Assertiveness is an interpersonal skill that describes a method of handling situations that allows you to put forward your own point of view and seek to gain your own advantage, without undermining or undervaluing other people's views. In considering approaches to a difficult situation, the two polarised extremes are aggression and submission. Aggression describes a strong confrontational approach, in which the only objective of the individual is to achieve their own aims regardless of the feelings of others. The opposite to this is the submissive

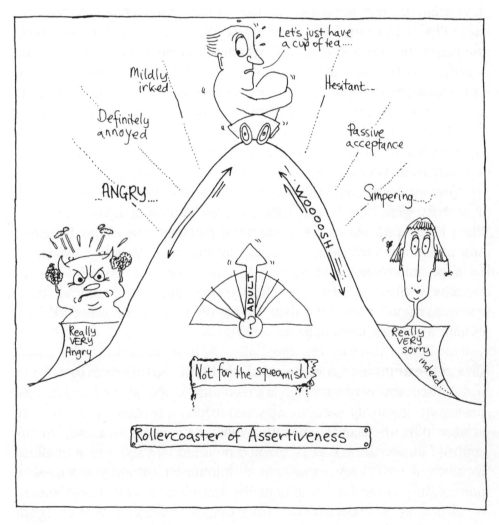

Figure 8 From aggression to submission: the rollercoaster of assertiveness

approach in which the individual 'gives in' to the views of the others regardless of their own desired outcome.

These descriptors highlight the opposite ends of a continuum, and there are many shades and varieties of responses in between. In fact, though we have a tendency towards one particular end of the range, we do vary from situation to situation. For example, an individual may be submissive at home, but an aggressive tyrant in the workplace. The skill in being assertive is to remain calm and in control, and this may require a lot of practice if a habitual approach is either to flare up or to back off. This can be developed by the use of calming techniques, such as controlled breathing. Also helpful is the use of appropriate body language, such as steady and unconfrontational eye contact, an open and undefensive posture, and the absence of distracting nervous gestures. Controlled breathing also produces a measured way of speaking that can convey an impressive clarity of thinking and a convincing certainty.

Verbal messages given in an assertive way consist of validating components as well as a clear statement of feelings or intentions. Such a message acknowledges the other person's feelings or action ('I appreciate that you are feeling upset'), but the second, and most important aspect, is that it states calmly your own feelings, desired actions or purpose. Without this clear statement, it can be easy to capitulate to the distress or anxieties of another, and subsequent actions may be fudged, watered-down or shelved indefinitely.

Imagine as a fairly new health- or social care student being challenged by a client who aggressively demands to be cared for by a qualified member of staff, as in their opinion you are not satisfactory as you are 'only a student'. The aggressive response would be to shout back ('It's not your place to question my authority! I'll get my boss to sort you out!') The submissive approach is to look upset and back off ('I knew I'd never be good enough!'). The assertive approach would be to acknowledge the client's concerns, while at the same time maintaining control ('I understand that you would prefer to be treated by a qualified member of staff. I am competent to administer the care you need at present, or you can wait until a qualified member of staff is available.')

It sounds a straightforward approach, but like all new skills needs practice and refinement. Once mastered, it can provide an invaluable bedrock of self-worth and confidence, which can help you navigate your way through the most turbulent of situations.

Handling and resolving conflict

Conflict will occur at some point in any collaborative venture (see Chapter 11). Some team members will view any kind of conflict negatively, and use it as evidence to support the view that collaboration is impossible or a waste of time. However, how conflict is recognised and how it is handled and resolved, is very important to the development of a team.

Social conflict theorists such as Georg Simmel in the early 1900s described conflict as pervasive in society, and suggested that it can help produce unity (Simmel, 1904). Coser, in 1956, developed these ideas and considered that as long as the social structure is open and flexible, and that the key issues causing conflict are not central to the working of the group, conflict can be construed as a necessary developmental phase. Therefore, it is important to acknowledge that conflict will occur, and to see it is a potential for development (Sands *et al,* 1990).

In resolving conflict, all the interpersonal skills previously discussed, such as attending, active listening, giving and receiving feedback, and assertiveness, will be required. In the process of conflict resolution, members of a team may adopt the aggressive or submissive approaches previously described. The most 'powerful' members may use their influence to coerce others into agreeing with them by being aggressive, whereas the less 'powerful' members of the group may bow to the strongest and most forcefully stated views. Neither of these approaches helps collaboration in terms of consensus decision-making and arriving at a pragmatic solution that all team members can support.

A middle-ground approach may be the way forward, serving as a compromise between a wide range of views. However, truly egalitarian compromises are difficult to achieve, and the team may not collectively 'own' the final decision, and not feel sufficiently committed to ensure its successful implementation. If an exchange of ideas and views has taken place in an open forum, with everyone's opinions being acknowledged, an objective decision should be possible without total warfare or absolute surrender. 'Under such circumstances, the team would be able to recognise conflict as an opportunity for growth and integration rather than a win-lose situation.' (Sands *et al*, 1990)

If we are to demonstrate that collaboration is effective, we all need to be aware of, and develop the skills of, interpersonal communication, so that we are more effective both as individuals and as members of a team. As with the fundamentals of mutual trust and respect, interpersonal communication is not a series of 'tick the box' skills that are simply acquired but never used. In order to develop an appropriate repertoire of interpersonal communication skills that are constructive for multi-professional collaboration, we need to accept that a process of refinement is both necessary and continual. 'The secret for accomplishing the art of effective communication is practice, practice, practice' (Phillips, 1992).

Summary of key points
- A basic level of communication demands each of us to attend to and listen to what others say.
- Being assertive means putting forward your own views and ideas without denigrating those of other people.
- Working appropriately through conflict can be developmental for the team working collaboratively.
- Communication skills have to be practised.

Action plan: demonstrating collaboration – the essentials

- How can you develop/enhance your understanding of interpersonal communication? Based on the SMART criteria for setting objectives (see Introduction, pxix) devise an action plan to achieve a quality improvement in your everyday practice.

Personal/professional goal

Service/organisational goal

Thinking time: an opportunity to reflect on the essentials of collaboration

1 Identify one situation in which you know you react either aggressively or submissively. This does not have to be a major life event. Perhaps you find it difficult returning faulty items to a shop, or refusing a poorly cooked meal at a restaurant.

2 Practise your response to one of these situations. Practise speaking calmly and clearly in front of a mirror while observing your body language. Observe your eye contact/posture/nervous gestures.

3 Have a go in the real situation.

4 Reflect on how it went.

5 Did you achieve the desired outcome?   Yes/No

6 Do you feel better about how you managed the situation?   Yes/No

7 In your opinion, did the person you dealt with feel upset or cross as a result of your actions?   Yes/no

8 Remember this approach will take time to develop, and reflection will help you identify what worked and what did not.

9 Identify another similar or different situation and try again.

CHAPTER 16

The Requisites: Teamworking Skills

HAVING CONSIDERED THE FUNDAMENTALS AND essentials of collaboration, it is now time to take a closer look at the requisites of multi-professional working. Teamworking skills – the ability to work harmoniously and productively with others towards a common goal – can be viewed as the necessary 'glue' that holds other collaborative skills in place. After all, trusting and respecting others (Chapter 14) and effective interpersonal communication (Chapter 15) could be argued to be key to professional practice *per se*, regardless of whether you are an autonomous practitioner working in the community or a core member of a multi-disciplinary team working within a hospital-based clinical speciality.

However, it is the interconnectedness of teamwork that makes any multi-professional project truly collaborative, in the sense that it is a shared enterprise from inception through to delivery to evaluation. Although we may all work with groups of people, it is a common purpose and the focus this brings that produces a 'team' from an *ad hoc* assembly of individuals (Rowe, 1996).

Defining teamwork

There is no doubt that the boundaries that differentiate collaboration from teamwork are not always fixed or transparent, and that a shared core of characteristics seems to lie at the heart of all effective interprofessional working (Headrick *et al*, 1998, see Table 15). Even if the characteristics pertinent for teamworking and collaboration share strong similarities, teams can be seen more as the organisational interface within a service or department, whereas collaboration encompasses a method of working that may be innovative and across traditional boundaries (Hart & Fletcher, 1999).

Another conundrum is to define exactly what a 'team' is, and indeed whether 'teamwork' itself is a mere illusion (Barr, 1997), or a phenomenon that defies precise description (Tierney & Vallis, 1999). Given the extreme variety of clinical settings, the differences in team structures and the infinite variations of multidisciplinary membership, perhaps it is impossible to describe a 'typical' team (Proctor-Childs *et al*, 1998). However, without a shared understanding of teamwork, multidisciplinary teams may be less effective in practice and unable to harness the full potential of collaborative working (While & Barriball, 1999).

A simple answer would be to say that a team is made up of the professional colleagues you encounter in an average working day, and

Table 15 *The A, B, C and D of multi-professional working (based on Headrick et al, 1998)*

A Achievable goals/objectives
- Shared and viable across disciplines/agencies
- Client- or service-focused

B Basic communication competence
- Interpersonal and IT skills
- Appropriate and facilitative systems, and protocols

C Cooperation
- Mutual trust and respect
- Synergy of skills, attributes, knowledge and experience

D Dynamic
- Flexible and adaptable team members
- Flexible and adaptable management and organisation

that teamworking is little more than talking with them and getting on with 'business as usual'. However, there is a marked difference between a collection of individuals working together or 'networking', and the shared identity, aims, commitments and methods of a fully functioning team. It can be easy to assume that if you bring together a number of practitioners they magically transform into a 'team'. Evidently, there is more to being in a team than just the designation of a collective noun: 'The belief that one could bring together a multi-professional group of people and simply expect them to provide effective teamwork seems somewhat naïve' (Miller *et al*, 1999).

The need for teamwork

Part of the problem is that we all like to feel wanted and included, again relating back to Maslow's theory of human motivation and the need to belong and be loved (Maslow, 1987) (see Chapter 6). The ethos of teams and teamwork pervades so much of the media, the academic literature and social policies that it raises expectations that we should all need and want to work within a 'team', and that this is a desirable way to practise. Some of you may recall childhood experiences in the school playground when teams were being picked for rounders or football. There was always one child chosen by neither side, who was left waiting to be picked reluctantly by the side who was just one short of a complete team. How crushing that feeling of not being wanted must have been, and how humiliating it must have felt not being eagerly embraced into a team (perhaps you were that child!).

It is evident that teams are not confined to health- and social care settings, but are prevalent in industry, business, sport and other competitive activities. Taking the example of a football team, the notion of a 'team' can be seen very much in the context of a shared identity (same kit or strip); shared commitment (team-training and tactics), and shared aims (to score goals and to win matches). Not all these characteristics translate well into a health- and social care setting, but it is apparent that embodied in the title of 'team' is a sense of collegiate spirit and communal enthusiasm for accomplishment.

With so much positive press, it is hard to argue the case for the merits of working as an independent autonomous practitioner (Headrick *et al*,

1998). However, working in a multi-professional team may suit some clinical areas and client groups better than others. The literature does offer some excellent examples of specialist areas, or particular services, where teamworking seems to produce an integrated and holistic approach to care, but this may not be transferable to all health- and social care settings (Hickling, 2000; Miller, 2000; Proctor-Childs *et al*, 1998; Swanson, 1997).

Purpose and membership

Broome (1998) argues that 'teamwork should be designed selectively', and that teams are best suited to working on projects where there is a degree of uncertainty. Here, the shared vision, purpose and values that teamworking may generate can enhance its ability to come to a consensus creatively and effectively. Broome (1998) also points out that for relatively technical tasks with a high degree of certainty, then teamworking is something of a luxury. Although teams can be a mutually supportive way of working, they can also have particular stresses and tensions that are simply not there if you work on your own in splendid isolation.

The reality is that working in a team is a common experience for today's health- and social care practitioner. The problems encountered by clients and their families are too complex, and require such variable amounts of time to identify and address that no one profession or practitioner can be an effective 'one-stop shop'. However, another reality is that today's practitioner may be a member of several different teams simultaneously, each with different histories, purposes and cultures – for example, a profession-specific team and a clinical speciality team. It is also the case that we cannot choose who our team colleagues are, the hard truth being that we have to find a tolerable way of working within the context of the team or teams that shape our professional responsibilities and match our job descriptions (Headrick *et al*, 1998).

Even if multi-professional teams are a well established way of working in a particular area, then team stability and consistency of outcomes can come under enormous pressure. Team membership may be in a continual state of flux due to the normal cycle of personnel joining and leaving posts (Hart & Fletcher, 1999). Teams may also consist of part-time workers or personnel who are on fixed contracts, or work shifts, or who are on rotational posts or are newly qualified (While & Barriball, 1999). Equally, the work of the team may be influenced by organisational factors such as service restructuring, or by the directives of social policy or legislation. In this context of perpetual variation, the golden ideal of 'teamwork' can be difficult to actually achieve and demanding to maintain (Finlay, 2000).

Describing teamwork

The actual structure of teams can vary, ranging across a broad spectrum from informal, occasional teams to more formal, highly organised methods of working (Headrick *et al*, 1998). There is no one universal blueprint for the ideal team, and Ovretveit (1996) has described the different kinds of teams using five dimensions, as shown in Table 16.

Table 16 *Dimensions of teamwork*

1 Degree of integration
How closely together does the team work?

2 Extent of collective responsibility
Who is accountable?
How are resources managed?

3 Membership
Informal attenders or committed regulars?

4 Client pathway and decision-making
How does the team deliver care or a service?

5 Management structures
How is the team managed?

Each team may have its own unique combination of some, if not all, of these descriptors, and you may be able to identify the particular configuration of your current team. The descriptors may also help you to compare and contrast the different teams you have worked in, past and present, and to identify their relative strengths, inefficiencies and complexities. The membership of a team is a significant influence on multi-professional collaboration: to be effective, a number of factors need to be considered in order to deliver integrated care. The variables of skills mix, age, gender and status can all impact on effective team functioning, best described by Balzer Riley (2000) as a 'pot-pourri' of differences. (See Table 17.)

Table 17 *The who, how and what of teamwork (based on Ovretveit, 1996)*

Variations in team membership:

Personnel: who?
• Professional mix
• Support staff mix
• Managerial mix

Distinction: how often?
• Core (full-time team member)
• Associate (part-time team member)

Skills: what can they do?
• Profession-specific
• Generic
• Individual/specialised

Socio-environmental: what influences what they do?
• Age
• Gender
• Personal beliefs and values
• Status or seniority
• Size of team
• Location and accessibility of team base

Teamworking skills

If you do operate within a team, what skills are required to keep the team functioning, and to achieve multi-professional collaboration? Broome (1998) lists the characteristics of a functioning team and sees them as consisting primarily of interpersonal skills, such as individual members caring for each other, and being open and truthful (see Chapters 14 and

15). Broome also cites team commitment and consensus as a sign of a functioning team. This can be reflected by a team's sense of shared responsibility for devising and delivering services that may encompass fraught times, as well as more settled, uneventful times.

Miller *et al* (1999) cite the notion of being a 'team player' as a key attribute for a team member, and that a learning culture needs to pervade a team, enabling an inter-professional exchange of skills. The concept of a 'team player' is an interesting one, as we can all think of examples of people with whom we have worked, who consider themselves to be 'in a team'. However, when demands intensify and deadlines draw nearer, such people often bail out of any concerted team effort, often citing more pressing personal or uni-professional commitments. Being a 'team player' therefore requires a commitment that transcends individual goals and agendas, undeniably having a profound impact on our distinct professional identities and sense of self.

Other teamworking skills can include the ability to be flexible and to respect different perspectives that may exist between team members. Equally important is the ability to be clear about your distinct contribution to the team. Miller *et al* (1999) refer to this as 'disciplinary articulation' – that is, the ability to explain your role and unique professional skills, as well as being aware of areas of role overlap.

To do this with confidence requires you not only to be clear about your own professional remit, but to have some appreciation of the role and

---

'In their own words': characteristics of teamwork

Teamwork:
- Requires a commitment to the philosophy of working together.
- Needs a positive attitude and a constructive approach.
- Should avoid whinges about workloads and systems.
- Is being reflexive about practice.
- Needs an interdisciplinary approach to education.
- Means you need to understand your own and other professional roles.
- Is being prepared to lead or support.
- Is working towards agreeing on team goals and responsibilities.
- Should have an active awareness of all the barriers to collaboration.

responsibilities of other disciplines, so that common ground can be a fruitful source of collaborative working and not a reason for conflict. Proctor-Childs *et al* (1998) describe this as 'a high level of role understanding', which can appear daunting to a new team member who is struggling to make sense of their own role within the team, let alone have an in-depth understanding of other professional roles. The key here is a willingness to learn and understand, and not that each of us should be the fount of all knowledge about all disciplines in all health- and social care settings. Barr (1998) describes these abilities as 'collaborative competencies' that can characterise functioning collaborative teams (see Table 18).

Table 18 *Collaborative competencies (based on Barr, 1998)*

Common – generic interpersonal and ethical competencies that underpin professional practice.

Complementary – profession-specific competencies that contribute to client-centred goal-setting.

Collaborative – competencies that enhance multi-professional working, such as role clarity and teamwork.

Confident communication is central to being able to articulate clearly what we do, but it is not just a case of using relevant interpersonal skills. Specifically, the language we use to define and describe our professional role may not be precise enough to promote a better multidisciplinary understanding. A potential source of confusion is terms or concepts that are interpreted in different ways across professional groups. A term such as 'activities of daily living' may sound straightforward enough, but how it is understood and applied may vary according to your professional background. Important concepts, such as the notion of 'care' and 'holistic practice' may also be subject to different professional interpretations (Owen & Holmes, 1993; Phillips, 1993). These key concepts and terms are often embedded in profession-specific theories or 'cognitive maps' (Miller *et al,* 1999), and are often central to a profession's identity and philosophic tenets (see also Chapters 13 and 15).

Therefore, a key skill in teamwork is making sure that everyone is clear about what is being discussed, and being prepared to unravel possible multiple meanings in commonly used terms. This requires patience and fortitude in order to arrive eventually at a shared understanding that does not pander or patronise. As Barr notes, if this is not achieved, then the team may be built on unstable foundations that may subside at a crucial time. 'Unfortunately, the use of common words and phrases gives the appearance of agreement and understanding between the team members; however, this is often superficial. The confusion comes to light when it becomes necessary to make complex decisions' (Barr, 1997).

Developing a team

There also has to be some acknowledgement that teams, and concomitantly 'teamworking', evolve over time and do not just naturally occur overnight because professions are grouped together due to ward or departmental organisation (Tierney & Vallis, 1999). Keeping a consistent team membership can be problematic, as mentioned earlier; for example, constant changes in personnel can reduce teamwork to the lowest common denominator, that of daily survival and 'firefighting'.

In addition, how members join and leave a team can contribute to the overall health of the team culture. Any change in membership may require some sort of transitory process. This may encompass a phasing-in or out of work tasks and responsibilities, and a social 'rites of passage' to mark an individual's contribution to the collective whole. Balzer Riley (2000) describes the developmental phases of an evolving team as a journey from childhood to adulthood. The phases include four stages – of 'forming' (childhood); 'storming' (adolescence); 'norming' (young adulthood) and to 'performing' (adulthood). Based on the work of Tuckman (1965), it provides a framework for noticing, understanding and working through the ways in which groups of people learn to work together.

It is important to accept that any team may need to get through periods of uncertainty and testing out ('forming' and 'storming'), and experience tension in clarifying particular roles, including leadership ('storming'), before being able to achieve multi-professional collaboration. All too often teams struggle under unrealistic expectations to 'perform' and deliver the 'goods', without an acknowledgement of how important earlier phases of team development are to a productive outcome. Helping a team through these stages of development may require the investment of time, resources and organisational support, as well as team-building initiatives at critical growth points of a team (Barr, 1997).

Teams are a complex and challenging way of delivering health- and social care, and require a formidable range of skills to keep a team at a level of optimal functioning. However, the onus is not on one team member alone to do this, but is a shared endeavour and very much a

Figure 9 Developmental stages of an evolving team

'In their own words': explaining teamwork

'Training is important – knowing how people learn and their strengths and weaknesses. Better to build up people's strengths than focus on their weaknesses – devolve those tasks to others.'

'team effort'. Certain factors can propel a team forwards, such as enabling and supportive management as well as skilled and creative leadership (Hart & Fletcher, 1999) (see Chapter 12). Given the impetus that change has within our working lives, how teams perform over time is also significant. Changes in working practices and the demands of needs-led services require teams to be responsive and often pro-active to change. Broome (1998) talks of the management of complex change requiring a 'critical mass of significant people', defining a critical mass as 'the least number to make the change happen'. It could be that it may be more productive to consider how collaborative interprofessional teams initiate and manage change, than to become too introspectively focused on 'teamworking' *per se*. 'There is a need for a responsive workforce to rise to the challenges proposed by current health needs. Multi-disciplinary team collaboration could be a reality rather than a myth, if the organisational ethos supports and aids collaboration, and individuals receive guidance to facilitate the process.' (Rowe 1996).

Summary of key points
- A team is a group of people who work together cooperatively and share a common purpose.
- Consistent teamwork in today's health- and social care services is under pressure, due to changing workforce patterns at local and national levels.
- Teams vary widely and may have differences of membership, organisation and management.
- Being a 'team player' may require you to show commitment and be clear about what attributes, skills and knowledge you have to contribute.
- Teams can evolve over time and can develop cooperative ways of working. The pro-active management of change may be a better indicator of effectiveness than 'teamworking' *per se*.

155

Action plan: demonstrating collaboration – the requisites

- How can you develop/enhance your understanding of teamwork and teamworking skills? Based on the SMART criteria for setting objectives (see Introduction, pxix), devise an action plan to achieve a quality improvement in your everyday practice.

Personal/professional goal

Service/organisational goal

Thinking time: an opportunity to reflect on the requisites of collaboration

1 Complete a SWOT analysis (strengths, weaknesses, opportunities and threats). From your own perspective, identify the positive and negative aspects of teamwork (think of a recent clinical experience where you observed or worked as part of a team).

Strengths	Weaknesses
Opportunities	**Threats**

2 Complete a SWOT analysis for your particular health- or social care discipline.

Strengths	Weaknesses

Opportunities	Threats

Having completed the SWOT analyses as a 'brainstorming' exercise, identify ONE personal strength and ONE professional opportunity you can develop further.

3 Brainstorm a list of team-building activities appropriate for your workplace and clinical setting:

For example:
- Skills-teaching across disciplines
- Inter-professional study sessions/days addressing a common need
- Team 'away days' to discuss long-term strategies
- Journal clubs
- Shared feedback from conferences
- Shared calendar/timetable of events
- Shared notice or bulletin board
- Access to a range of professional journals and texts
- Multi-professional case reviews
- Students on placement from across a range of disciplines
- Multi-professional 'open days' for other staff/departments/the public
- Social events.

4 Think about how staff join, remain in and leave your team (or a team you have worked in recently). Use the following checklist to determine the 'health' of your team:

Joining a team – introductions
- Is there an induction process?
- Are short-term expectations clear?
- Are long-term expectations clear?
- What support is available: who? when? where?

Staying in a team, communication network (formal, informal)
- What are the methods for information exchange?
- Is giving and receiving feedback customary practice?
- Who is included in decision-making, and how?
- What stability factors are there, in terms of providing continuity and certainty?
- Is there room for attention to personal details and acknowledging individual talents and skills?
- Is the 'human touch' evident? (Appropriate use of humour, empathy or pragmatism).

Leaving a team – handover of role
- Is there a timetable to manage the devolving of tasks and responsibilities?
- Is the process of disengagement being acknowledged?
- Has 'succession planning' been considered?
- Are there appropriate opportunities for informal/formal 'goodbyes'?

CHAPTER **17**

The Obligations: Roles and Responsibilities

THE AIM OF THIS CHAPTER IS TO identify some of the obligations that impact upon our collaborative decision-making in professional practice. These obligations focus primarily on our professional codes of conduct and the ethical basis for professional decision-making. There are also other factors at a local level of policy that influence our clinical decision-making and the remit of our professional roles. The workplace or organisation itself may have developed quite specific guidelines as to what roles are acceptable in practice for each profession. However, there are other less explicit professional obligations that are socially and culturally determined. In other words, professional roles and responsibilities are shaped by different levels of external demands and expectations.

The purpose of professional bodies

Every profession has specific characteristics that include possessing a unique body of knowledge; a set of rules or a code of conduct based on acknowledged ethical principles, and the ability to discipline members who contravene those rules (professional misconduct).

The purpose of a professional body is to maintain a list of those registered in the profession, providing a licence to practice. It requires practitioners to maintain their professional competence through educational updating; advises government on legislation and social policy, and exists in all of these functions to protect the public. The regulatory body that consists of a group of professionals, has statutory legislation, passed by Parliament, that sets out the requirements for the regulation of professional practice in order to protect clients (College of Occupational Therapists, 2000).

Ethical and moral dilemmas in practice can arise all too frequently, and professional judgement is required at every stage of the decision-making process in order to ensure that the needs and wishes of clients are paramount. Practitioners look to their professional codes to find the ethical guidance they need, but in an environment of changing roles and shifting boundaries, practice today may be constantly testing the established 'rules' (see also Chapters 4 and 13).

The professional codes of conduct

Within multi-professional collaboration, practitioners may be aware of colleagues from a range of healthcare disciplines being accountable to different codes of conduct. It can be beneficial to appreciate the similarities and differences embodied in different professional codes of conduct, and how this can impinge on the roles and responsibilities of team colleagues. This enhances a realistic understanding of the complex nature of clinical decision-making, and can often explain the different perspectives and emphasis of values of multidisciplinary colleagues. Although this sounds like common sense in theory, we can get so immersed in our own profession's code of conduct and what is 'sacrosanct', that we tend to forget or overlook the professional parameters of others.

For example, a common team dilemma occurs when professionals disagree over the amount of information a client should be given about their biomedical condition, particularly if the client is frail and other family members do not wish them to be told any bad news. Alternatively, there is the classic challenging dilemma of whether or not a client should be resuscitated. The exact threshold point when the focus of practitioners changes from preserving life and escalating treatment to keeping the client comfortable and preparing them for a dignified death is a matter for professional judgement, and is not signposted by irrefutable absolutes.

When all practitioners are accountable for their actions to their respective professional bodies, individual interpretation of professional codes can lead to a crisis of accountability and a stalemate in collaborative decision-making. The danger here is that inertia can occur, and each professional group may become paralysed by perceived responsibilities or, worse, consider their ethical stance as superior to that of other colleagues. To keep the wheels of multi-professional collaboration turning, open discussion is paramount in order to arrive at a pragmatic solution that has moral integrity and the support of the whole team. An example of meeting such a horned dilemma straight on, and achieving an outcome, was the collaborative statement issued by the nursing and medical colleges in the UK to guide practice and clarify professional responsibilities for *Do Not Resuscitate Orders* (Royal College of Nursing and the British Medical Association, 1993).

The professional remit for collaboration

When working within health- and social care, there are bound to be commonly recurring altruistic values that unite the many strands of multi-professional practice. However, codes of conduct across professional groups may vary on how such values are defined, described and weighted. Consequently, there are some interesting variations across codes of conduct, which are more a case of emphasis rather than vast moral wastelands (see also Chapter 4).

Looking at examples within the UK, the Chartered Society of Physiotherapy (CSP) calls physiotherapists to 'communicate and co-operate with colleagues and avoid criticism of them'. Also, there is no educational obligation stated in their code, but it does include recommendations for appropriate liability cover (Chartered Society of Physiotherapy, 1996).

Occupational therapists (OTs) are given specific guidance for the accurate recording of client information, and are asked to involve only one therapist in the care of an individual unless a second opinion is sought. The code also highlights the necessity of 'respecting needs, traditions, competence and responsibilities' of other professions as part of their own professional practice (College of Occupational Therapists, 2000). Although nurses are charged with working in a collaborative and co-operative manner, while recognising and respecting other healthcare

163

professionals and their contribution to the team, they do not specifically allude to consideration of the traditions and responsibilities of other professionals (UKCC, 1992a & b). However, common to these codes is the underscoring of accountability for any professional action or delegated work, and a focus on the delivery of care and service provision to clients.

Promoting collaboration by developing joint standards

A closer look at professional frameworks reveals many more shared similarities than differences. An example within the UK of a collaborative project is the work begun between the United Kingdom Central Council (UKCC for nursing, midwifery and health visiting) and the General Medical Council (GMC for doctors) to promote common standards for client care that could apply to practitioners registered with both Councils (UKCC, 2000). The aim is to adopt a more collaborative approach to defining public expectations of healthcare professionals within the health- and social care environment.

Promoting partnership through development of joint standards can be seen as a pro-active measure to support and strengthen collaboration between all health- and social care professionals engaged in practice and developing quality services. This also requires endeavours to explore the perspectives of each professional group, in order to make more explicit the ethical and philosophical basis for each profession's style and substance of decision-making. Clearly such a process needs mutual trust and respect as well as a climate of open communication (see Chapters 14 and 15).

Professional responsibilities and duties

To act professionally, practitioners are required to be ethically responsible for their actions. For example, the medical code ('Duties of a Doctor') focuses on a deontological approach to practice, by emphasising absolute duty, and delineated rights and wrongs of professional decision-making (General Medical Council, 2001). In the current climate, where rationing of care presents as an everyday pressure, how do professionals manage dilemmas of who gets what? Can one client's care be compromised to allow another client to receive even substandard care as opposed to nothing at all? If it is not deemed safe to admit another patient into an already overcrowded hospital ward, but there is literally no other place to go, what happens? Are the laudable principles of trying to provide the greatest good to the greatest number outweighed by the duty to provide some level of care to absolutely all those who need it?

A topical UK example of this is the winter bed crisis witnessed by intensive care units (ICUs) all over the country. This has become an annual pattern of events, now extending beyond the winter period, and is a very marked example of the rationing of resources and having to prioritise who gets what. Practitioners have to weigh up the risks of transferring out their most stable critically ill patients, so that the limited number of beds are available to the most acutely ill patients. Despite being stabilised, such a transfer may have clinical risks associated with it, and might not be in the best interests of an individual patient.

However, the alternative risks of managing a critically ill patient in an inappropriately equipped casualty resuscitation room are also a factor, given that such patients may need management in a specialised ICU environment in order to optimise their chance of survival. To admit a resuscitated patient, and to have access to the level of expert care in the ICU, could be cited as promoting the interests of that particular patient. Conversely, an argument could be made on the principle of equality of access and the need to promote better standards for critical care across the country for all those who need it. Risks are associated with each option, and assessing, managing and working with risks are part of the responsibilities of multi-professional practice.

Ethical principles and clinical decision-making

Commonly occurring ethical principles of doing good (beneficence) and doing no harm (non-maleficence) can be found or implied in all codes of conduct, and can be used to describe either consequence of the difficult clinical scenario described above. Many of the codes, although interestingly not the medical code, refer explicitly to the professional duty to report to an appropriate authority, circumstances that may put other patients at risk. Whichever decision was made, every attempt needs to be made by professionals to prevent untenable situations recurring to avoid putting patients at risk.

Another key ethical principle is respecting client autonomy, which is paramount in some codes and lower profile in others. Autonomy can be described as clients having control over their lives and their wishes, needs and interests being listened to when receiving care or accessing a service. Respecting autonomy may be an integral part of a practitioner's approach if clients are adults, verbally fluent and confident about asserting their views. Decisions can become difficult when the client is particularly young and immature, or old and particularly frail, or has limited experience in acting as an autonomous individual. This raises the question of how much capacity for logical thought and deliberation is needed to be considered as an autonomous agent. Professionals need to be equipped with the skills of assessment to make these often highly delicate decisions. This can usefully include the confidence to collaborate with team colleagues who are able to contribute sound professional judgement without acting with presumption or arrogance.

Justice is another key ethical principle, and this is synonymous with fairness. This can be in the form of distributive justice (in terms of allocating finite resources); rights-based justice (concerning the individual citizen), or legal justice (societal laws). Equality is at the heart of justice, though this can be difficult to operationalise in hugely varied and disparate client populations. Dilemmas can be a simple decision, from which patient gets the last clean sheet or pillow, to which patient receives the expensive drug therapy, the transplant or the one computerised tomography (CT) scan slot available that day?

It is clear from the previous examples of ethical principles that clinical decision-making in today's world is a complex process with no obvious easy answers. Professional responsibilities cannot be diminished or avoided, and the possible consequences of any course of action need to be fully explored. The final decision may not be the most palatable or instantly appealing, but should embody a pragmatic ethical soundness.

Clinical decision-making entails the constant juggling of ethical principles, requiring plans to be flexible in the light of the specific clinical context. This is difficult to sustain in the face of constant changes in clinical practice and service delivery, where professionals are striving to give accurate and consistent information to clients, carers and other members of the healthcare team. Prioritisation of care and clinical judgement in situations where resources are limited provides real challenges for the healthcare team. It requires discussion and reflection to ensure that all practitioners feel they are working in an ethically responsible way. The ethical principles of beneficence, non-maleficence, autonomy and justice need to provide a framework for making clinical decisions so that in collaborative practice practitioners can actively demonstrate accountability, as enshrined in their professional codes.

The influence of workplace cultures

It is important to recognise that practitioners are influenced in their decision-making by not only professional codes, but also by local policies and workplace guidelines (see Chapter 4). The influence of professional and workplace culture has been cited as exerting significant influence on professional decision-making. A UK example of this is an ethnographic study that examined the cultural and contextual factors that particularly affected nurses' decision-making, with respect to patient management decisions in an intensive care unit (Lovelady, 1998).

The themes that emerged from qualitative data analysis identified three distinct aspects to a workplace culture. These included the uni-professional culture, the specific unit culture (multi-professional team), and a socio-political ability (the practitioner's ability to identify and interpret a decision-making situation and influence others).

From this study, the uni-professional workplace culture revealed how nurses in particular perceived their own professional role in decision-making, and the role of other professionals involved in patient management. The perceptions included:

- The role of the nurse and reciprocal expectations
- Accountability
- Professional mandate to 'speak up' and 'go into battle'
- Dealing with the ramifications of the decision.

The latter three areas are involved with professionally determined roles, as advocated by the Code of Conduct. The first area touches upon more local beliefs. The issue of reciprocal role expectations relates to what is expected of each professional, and what is considered to be within the scope of their knowledge and expertise by themselves and others. When roles are shifting and healthcare practitioners are becoming increasingly autonomous with respect to traditional and more hierarchical practices, role confusion can feed interdisciplinary tension.

The expectation of a professional role from within and between professions is often more a subtle implication or pressure than a code of conduct, or a local or even workplace policy. It is more often the dynamics between professional groups that communicate the socially determined role expectations of professionals and the possibilities for multi-professional collaboration.

How practitioners are socialised or become 'enculturated' into their own particular profession can play a large part in these dynamics, and can convey implicit 'obligations' in the way teams work together. Professional enculturation is a process of social learning, giving the student or novice practitioner a 'rule' of how to behave. These 'rules' may be no more than acquired habits that may be no longer relevant to practice today, or be based on unhelpful and negative assumptions (see Chapter 13).

However, protocols and policies that have been devised by a multidisciplinary team provide 'rules' to govern practice in a particular clinical area, which ideally are theoretically sound and supported by the best available evidence. In-built into this clinical decision-making process is the opportunity to evaluate, revise, improve and move on. Although we all are susceptible to professional enculturation, we need to be mindful that this can entail acquiring 'bad' habits as well as good ones, and this can ultimately affect our ability and willingness to make the most of collaborative opportunities right under our noses.

'In their own words': explaining professional roles and responsibilities

- To know the 'bigger picture' and the remit of your colleagues, including senior management.
- To be aware of the pressures and stresses experienced by others.
- To know the roles and responsibilities of other professionals, and value them.
- To be willing to learn from good practice, from wherever it comes.

To challenge or comply?

Initially, the obligations that govern professional roles seem to be clearly laid out in the professional codes that are grounded in the ethical principles of beneficence, non-maleficence, autonomy and justice. All decisions need to be client-focused, and acknowledge and value the differing perspectives of a multi-professional team. Differences, where they exist, are a matter of emphasis rather than fundamentally polarised philosophical positions. However, practitioners also have to acknowledge the role-limitations imposed by local and workplace policy, and from statutory and legal obligations. Detailing generic and profession-specific responsibilities in clearly written policy documents or protocols avoids the onus on the individual practitioner of having to adopt a 'trial and error' approach to defining the parameters of practice.

Finally, the culture of an organisation and its influence on professional decision-making is not to be underestimated. This pressure is more subtle and rarely written, but typically communicated informally and formally through social interaction. It is important for practitioners to be aware of these potential influences and to decide for themselves whether to challenge them or comply with them. Such influences may promote or restrict contributions to multi-professional collaboration, and need to be open to objective scrutiny. The skills of self-awareness, insight and reflection help the practitioner to be constantly vigilant, and to operate in any clinical context with ethical integrity.

Summary of key points

- Professional practice is governed by codes of conduct for each profession, set down by professional bodies to which they are accountable. These codes embody the ethical principles of beneficence, non-maleficence, autonomy and justice.
- Local policy and workplace policy/guidelines further augment or limit professional roles.
- The influence of professional and particularly workplace cultures subtly conveys further expectations of role performance through social interaction within and between professions.

Action plan: demonstrating collaboration – the obligations

- How can you develop/enhance your understanding of your role and professional responsibilities? Based on the SMART criteria of setting objectives (see Introduction, pxix), devise an action plan to achieve a quality improvement in your everyday practice.

Personal/professional goal

Service/organisational goal

Thinking time: an opportunity to reflect on the obligations of collaborative working

1 Look again at your own code of conduct. Actively seek out the codes of conduct of other health- and social care professionals in your team or organisation, in order to compare and contrast.

2 Identify how your code of conduct priorities integrate with your job description, and your last appraisal plan with your department or service objectives.

3 Think of two recent clinical decisions. What ethical principles underpinned your decision, and how does your code of conduct support your professional judgement?

4 Think of a conflict situation within your team or organisation concerning a recent clinical decision. What did each professional use as evidence to support their position, and what ethical principles/ aspects of their code of conduce did these involve?

5 Think of any local or workplace policies that you might have encountered, and their influence on your practice. Did you feel there were any conflicts of interest that highlighted an ethical issue?

6 Think back to when you started work in your current environment.
   • How did you learn how to function in that environment? (How did you 'learn the ropes'?)
   • Did anything surprise of unnerve you? Why?
   • What did you do to challenge or comply with the situation?
   • What were the consequences?

CHAPTER 18

The Commitments: Seeing it Through and Making it Work

A RECURRING THEME THROUGHOUT this guide to collaborative working has been to acknowledge some of the very real practical difficulties, but to remain positive, even optimistic, about the benefits of collaborative working. A serious critique of the drawbacks and deficiencies of this way of working in an ever-changing and complex health- and social care arena is not the primary function of this book. However, a pragmatic approach to change does need to acknowledge that despite all the groundwork and good intentions, staying with a collaborative project takes determination and belief in a long-term vision.

By asking ourselves if collaboration works, we beg the question of what we mean by 'works', and what do we really expect from changing our working practices? As health- and social care professionals, do we feel compelled to improve our practice and the interactions we have with our clients, and will we endeavour to try out a whole range of interventions and policies, big or small, in the pursuit of 'getting it better'?

One thing that is guaranteed is that if we do not know what 'works', or how we expect it to manifest itself, change within health- and social care will continue apace. As stated by Wheeler and Grice (2000):'Health and Social care provision is in a state of permanent change. It may be tempting to look forward to the time when it all settles down; however there is no reason to believe that it will and, therefore, good clinicians must perform in a constantly changing environment'.

Achieving goals and indicators of success

Wheeler and Grice (2000) propose certain 'ingredients' for coping with the process of change, including early experiences of the benefits of change. Early signs that changed ways of working have a discernible impact on practice are crucial to maintaining motivation and morale. Goals for collaboration that are set too far in the future, or have no short-term markers for success at all, can be a deflating, despairing experience.

Proving collaboration works is undoubtedly a complex enterprise. If collaborative practice relies on cooperation between different disciplines and agencies, this interdependency can be hard to measure. The goals of collaborative projects may also be focused on quality improvements in services, so therefore quantitative measures and statistical analysis may not fully capture what has been achieved in terms of the clients' experience of health- and social care.

Recent projects have endeavoured to address these issues by adopting imaginative and comprehensive ways of evaluating change, both qualitatively and quantitatively. For example, Reeves (2000b) described a pilot education project for pre-registration house officers (PRHOs) and newly qualified nurses. The project consisted of a series of lunchtime inter-professional education sessions, aimed at exploring shared clinical concerns using practical learning methods. Before and after questionnaires were used to evaluate the project, as well as using observational data noted during the sessions and an individual participant interview three months after the project had finished. Other examples of mixed method approaches to evaluating collaboration are evident in the literature, and indeed it can be argued that a variety of evaluation tools enables a more valid, multi-dimensional picture of the realities of collaboration to be built up (Ross *et al*, 2000).

Being able to evaluate collaboration and to actually demonstrate that real gains have been achieved, has to be an aim nurtured at the inception of the project. Bolt-on and hasty *ad hoc* evaluations rarely capture the process or true spirit of what was originally envisaged and delivered. As Wheeler and Grice (2000) noted, attention to the impact of change needs to be explored from the onset, and Reeves (2000b) argues that evaluation can play a 'crucial element' in a joint venture.

'Joined-up' problem-solving

Although these points support the notion of evaluation being considered and developed in parallel to the actual project itself, the time and effort involved in this is no doubt apparent to all practitioners and would-be researchers. However, perhaps we need to change our thinking and the way we develop projects and innovations. For example, UK government initiatives have advocated more 'joined up health and social care' (Department of Health, 2000b), and this may require not only 'joined-up' thinking but, more fundamentally, 'joined-up' problem-solving.

With this current wave of a more systematic and considered way of evaluating collaboration, it would be easy to think that the evidence that collaboration works would follow naturally, and with an abundant supply of concrete, unassailable facts. However, the road to proving collaboration 'works' may be more tortuous and protracted than that. For example, a recent systematic review of quantitative evidence for the effectiveness of inter-professional education concluded that there was a paucity of sufficiently rigorous studies and that, at present, no quantitative evidence exists on the effects of inter-professional education (Zwarenstein *et al*, 1999).

However, the review concludes that this need not mean abandoning all hope and discontinuing all interprofessional education immediately. Rather, a more circumspect view of effectiveness needs to be considered and pursued, and Zwarenstein *et al* (1999) state that no evidence of effectiveness: 'does not imply that there is evidence of ineffectiveness of interpersonal education, simply that no such evidence currently exists'.

Involving all 'stakeholders'

Adopting and skilfully using different evaluative tools is not the only consideration in proving that collaboration 'works'. Ensuring that the full range of view-points and stake-holder perspectives is adequately and appropriately represented is also crucial. The process of change and the impact of collaborative working may indeed result in different experiences for the practitioners, the clients, their carers and the service managers. Following a pedagogic project to ascertain a variety of stakeholders' opinions and expectations of multi-professional courses using a mixed method approach, Atkins *et al* (2000) noted that: 'the underpinning philosophy for this study supports both the user-orientated and the responsive approach. It includes consideration of human, contextual and strategic factors combined with sensitivity to multiple points of view'.

Finding methods of evaluation that are equally valid and reliable across the spectrum of health- and social care, both in practice and in education, is clearly a difficult task. The aim should be to explore and develop a repertoire of evaluation tools and systematic audits that can be used flexibly and that can complement each other. The question 'So, does collaboration work?' also needs to be refined, and this may help us choose more wisely an appropriate evaluation method that is fit for the purpose. What we really need to be asking ourselves, as practitioners and educators, is why a collaborative project might be appropriate; what may be the discernible impact on health- and social care delivery; what is the timescale of such changes, and is this approach worth the investment of time, resources and effort? If so, how might further refinements and changes to practice produce a more efficient service, and who will benefit from such improvements?

The future of multi-professional collaboration: from 'signposts' to maps

Learning to collaborate is not only about a willingness to explore and experiment, but also about learning to critically evaluate experiences. New ways of working are only synthesised into our existing professional practice if we feel they have utility, fit our personal and professional ideologies, and we are confident about how, and why, they work. In the Preface, we stated that this book was to act as a series of 'signposts' to collaborative working. It is now the shared responsibility of us all to develop detailed 'maps' of the how and why of collaborative working, to maintain professional standards and to promote health- and social care practice of the highest calibre.

Summary of key points

- Commitment to staying with a collaborative project is as key to its success as other factors, requiring determination and belief in a long-term vision.
- Focus initial indicators of change on short-term, achievable goals.
- Develop a strategy for evaluation and review in parallel to the 'nuts and bolts' of planning and implementing collaborative working.
- No single method of evaluation is ideal. Adopt a mixed method approach with a clear rationale, aiming to reflect the interests of the people and 'stakeholders' involved.

Action plan: demonstrating collaboration – seeing it through and making it work

- How can you contribute to seeing a collaborative project through and help to make it a success? Based on the SMART criteria of setting objectives (see Introduction, pxix), devise an action plan that would help to sustain a collaborative project in your everyday practice.

Personal/professional goal

Service/organisational goal

Go for it! What helps collaboration?
- Starting small and aiming for an achievable goal.
- Identifying your own contribution, both personally and professionally.
- Doing your homework and background research in advance to avoid reinventing the wheel.
- Defining your parameters ruthlessly: what time/resources/people are really available?
- Listening as well as talking, and being prepared to change your views.
- Sharing openly and discussing creatively.
- Being honest when you have got stuck/sied-tracked or gone 'off the boil', either individually or as a team.
- Setting up ways to monitor and check progress in the early stages.
- Valuing small indications of success and using them to promote the advantages of continuing to provide momentum for change.
- Rethinking and redirecting energies if a project is failing to meet its goals.
- Keeping it a challenge and not a chore.

(Adapted from Headrick *et al*, 1996)

What hinders collaboration?
- Not being prepared for the personal, professional and organisational complexities of collaboration.
- Being unrealistic about the timescales involved.
- Expecting too much too soon.
- Providing no additional 'pump priming' support, such as start-up funding, resources, time, staff.
- Allowing negative personal and professional differences to dominate.
- Not translating ideas, plans and/or policies into action.
- Fizzling out at the implementation stage.
- Losing heart at the monitoring and evaluation stage.
- Losing sight of the overall aim and the benefits of collaborative working.
- 'It is unlikely that there will be *one* single process of successful inter-professional collaboration. It is more likely that inter-professional developments between and within health and welfare groups will be variable and achieved in different ways between different sectors' Evetts (1999).

Getting started

Kick-starting your own efforts at collaborative working may require some personal stock-taking and some 'transformational change'.

Consider the following aspects of change, and see if you can identify the strengths and areas you need to consciously develop.

1 Change from being reactive to pro-active.
2 Change from the general to the specific.
3 Change from generating ideas to creating a formula for action.
4 Change from being politically unaware to being politically astute.
5 Change from being a 'can't do' to a 'can do' person.

(Based on the transformational changes, Sullivan, 1998).

'When we are part of a change whether forced upon us or not, it always involves some degree of loss. We say goodbye to the old ways, to ways we were familiar with and feel safe with, even though it might not have been a good place, it was familiar' (Jennison, 2001).

What is your attitude to change?

- How have you responded to changes in the past?
- How do you cope with short-term changes?
- How do you cope with long-term changes?
- How do you cope with organisational or professional changes?
- What are your personal 'triggers/alarm bells' that indicate you are not feeling comfortable with any proposed change?
- How did you respond to and cope with these 'triggers' in the past?
- How can you respond to and cope with these 'triggers' in the future?

APPENDIX

Integrated Case Study: An Example of Collaboration

This incident is based on a real-life situation; names have been changed to protect confidentiality and anonymity.

John
John had suffered a terrible injury when he was 21 years old, which had left him tetraplegic. Every day was very challenging for John and not easy for those caring for him. His anger and frustration were natural and coloured his ability to see that what we were doing was trying to help him. His family were devastated too and struggling to come to terms with John's loss for themselves, as well as supporting him. John became difficult to manage, with the team becoming more fragmented and providing even less consistent care. This exacerbated all of John's anxieties, as he received different messages from different people. As the team worked on John's rehabilitation to prepare him in the best way possible for the future, a core group of people actively formed together to provide consistent care for John. It was the most organised and sustained effort by the whole team. The occupational therapist, physiotherapist, pharmacist, a group of nurses and a doctor, all liaised often about how best to optimise John's physical and psychological

rehabilitation. The daily plan of therapy was complex and truly collaborative between the team and, eventually, John himself.

It was a long struggle through the storm and worst for John, of course, but once we were 'performing', the outcome was incredible and the celebration of each milestone, no matter how small to the outside world, was enormous. Target times on the tilt table and off the ventilator were celebrated, as well as John's ability to turn a page unaided and even contemplate the future again. Every achievement was a credit to John's courage, and those family members and professionals who worked together with him.

The inter-professional support and collaboration required to manage John's care illustrates that a team can work if health- and social care workers believe in the same goals and values, trust each other and communicate well. A lot of team learning took place, due to the diversity of expertise that was necessary to optimise John's care. It also reinforced the importance of valuing each distinct contribution to the collaborative process, and is an example of the satisfaction that can be gained from doing it well.

As an example of successful collaboration as measured by the patient, family and practitioners, can you identify the following from this case study in relation to the content in Chapters 14 to 18?

Fundamentals: mutual trust and respect
- Which relationships were key to John's rehabilitation?
- How was mutual trust and respect demonstrated?

Essentials: interpersonal communication
- What methods of communication were needed?
- What impact can distress, frustration, anger and anxiety have on interpersonal communication?
- How could you ensure that all individuals were able to communicate with each other at all stages of the treatment process?

Requisites: teamworking skills

- What were the most essential teamworking skills?
- How did they fix some of the initial problems?
- Imagine what the priorities of each team member (especially John and his family) may have been when considering a plan for care and rehabilitation: how can a team arrive at a consensus for action?

Obligations: roles and responsibilities

- Would there have been any overlap in roles and responsibilities in this case?
- What ethical issues might have influenced the care given to John?

Commitments: seeing it through and making it work

- How easy do you think it was, in practice, to maintain the level of commitment necessary to manage John's care?
- How important was it to celebrate small gains?
- How might a team cope with setbacks?
- Imagine how, in practice, you might organise your work to optimise those factors that facilitate collaboration.

References

Ames A, Adkins S, Rutledge D, Hughart K, Greeno S, Foss J, Gentry J & Trent M, 1992, 'Assessing Work Retention Issues', *Journal of Nursing Administration* 22(4), pp37–41.

Atkins J, 1998, 'Tribalism, Loss and Grief: Issues for Multi-Professional Education', *Journal of Interprofessional Care* 12(3), pp303–7.

Atkins J, Feaver S, Hall J, Hutchings S, List L, Sanders C & Skinner A, 2000, 'Stake Holder's Expectations of Multi-Professional Courses', School and Health Care Department of Professional Studies, with OCHRAD, Oxford Brookes University, unpublished pedagogic research report.

Baggs JG, 1994, 'Development of an Instrument to Measure Collaboration and Satisfaction about Care Decisions', *Journal of Advanced Nursing* 20, pp176–82.

Balzer Riley J, 2000, *Communication in Nursing*, 4th edn, Mosby, St Louis.

Barnes M & Warren L (eds), 1999, *Paths to Empowerment,* The Policy Press, Bristol.

Barr H, Hammick M, Kopppel I & Reeves S, 1999, 'Evaluating Interprofessional Education: Two Systematic Reviews for Health and Social Care', *British Educational Research Journal* 25(4), pp533–44.

Barr H & Waterton S, 1996, 'Summary of CAIPE Survey: Inter-Professional Education in Health and Social Care in the United Kingdom', *Journal of Interprofessional Care* 10(3), pp297–303.

Barr H, 1998, 'Competent to Collaborate: Towards a Competency-Based Model for Interprofessional Education', *Journal of Interprofessional Care,* 12(2), pp181–7.

Barr H, 2000a, 'New NHS, New Collaboration, New Agenda for Education', *Journal of Interprofessional Care* 14(1), pp81–6.

REFERENCES

Barr H, 2000b, 'Working Together to Learn Together: Learning Together to Work Together', *Journal of Interprofessional Care* 14(2), pp177–9.

Barr O, 1997, 'Interdisciplinary Teamwork: Consideration of the Challenges', *British Journal of Nursing* 6(17), pp1005–10.

Bee H, 1994, *Lifespan Development*, Harper Collins, New York.

Belbin RM, 1993, *Team Roles at Work*, Butterworth-Heinnemann, Oxford.

Bevan S, 1987, *The Management of Labour Turnover*, IMS Report 137, University of Sussex Institute of Manpower Studies.

Bevan S, Barber D & Robinson D, 1997, *Keeping the Best: A Practical Guide to Retaining Key Employees*, IES Report 337, Institute of Employment Studies, Brighton.

Braye S & Preston-Shoot M, 2000, 'Keys to Collaboration', in Davies C, Finlay L & Bullman A (eds), *Changing Practice in Health and Social Care*, SAGE Publications, London.

Broome A, 1998, *Managing Change*, 2nd edn, Macmillan, London.

Buchan J & Pike G, 1989, *PAMs into the 1990s – Professions Allied to Medicine: The Wider Labour Market Context*, University of Sussex, Institute of Manpower Studies.

Buchan J, Bevan S & Atkinson J, 1988, *Costing Labour Wastage in the NHS*, University of Sussex, Institute of Manpower Studies.

Burnard P, 1989, *Teaching Interpersonal Skills*, Chapman Hall, London.

Busby A & Gilchrist B, 1992, 'The Role of the Nurse in the Medical Ward Round', *Journal of Advanced Nursing* 17, pp339–46.

Calomeni CA, Solberg LI & Conn SA, 1999, 'Nurses on Quality Improvement Teams: How Do They Benefit?', *Journal of Nursing Care Quality* 13(5), pp75–96.

Cameron A & Masterson A, 1998, 'The Changing Policy Context of Occupational Therapy', *British Journal of Occupational Therapy* 61(12), pp556–60.

Candy P, Crebert G & O'Leary J, 1994, *Developing Lifelong Learners Through Undergraduate Education*, National Board of Employment, Education and Training (NBEET), Canberra.

Chartered Society of Physiotherapy, 1996, *Rules of Professional Conduct*, CSP, London.

Chartered Society of Physiotherapy, 2000, *Paper no CPD(00)31 Recent Developments and On-Going Work Relating to CPD/Lifelong Learning and Competence*, CSP, London.

Cherniss C, 1995, *Beyond Burnout: Helping Teachers, Nurses, Therapists and Lawyers Recover from Stress and Disillusionment*, Routledge, New York.

Christensen J, 1993, *Nursing Partnership – A Model for Nursing Practice,* Churchill Livingstone, Edinburgh.

Christman L, 1991, 'Perspectives on Role Socialisation of Nurses', *Nursing Outlook* 39(5), pp209–12.

Clark PG, 1994, 'Social, Professional and Educational Values on the Interdisciplinary Team: Implications for Gerontology and Geriatric Education', *Education Gerontology,* 20, pp35–51.

Clark PG, 1997, 'Values in Healthcare Profession Socialisation: Implications for Geriatric Education and Multidisciplinary Teamwork', *The Gerontologist* 37(4), pp441–51.

Clouder L, 2000, 'Reflective Practice: Realising its Potential', *Physiotherapy* 86(10), pp517–22.

Coeling HVE & Cukr PL, 2000, 'Communication Styles That Promote Perceptions of Collaboration, Quality and Satisfaction', *Journal of Nursing Care Quality* 14 (2), pp63–74.

Cohen R & Sampson J, 1999, 'Working Together: Students Learning Collaboratively', Higgs J & Edwards H (eds), *Educating Beginning Practitioners,* Butterworth-Heinemann, Oxford.

College of Occupational Therapists, 2000, *Code of Ethics and Professional Conduct for Occupational Therapists*, COT, London.

Cooley C, 2000, 'Communication Skills in Palliative Care: Part 4', *Professional Nurse* 15(9), pp603–5.

Coser LA, 1956, *The Functions of Social Conflict*, The Free Press of Glencoe.

Covey SR, 1989, *The 7 Habits of Highly Effective People,* Simon & Schuster, London.

Craik C, Austin C, Chacksfield JD, Richards G & Schell D, 1998, 'College of Occupational Therapists: Position Paper on the Way Ahead for Research, Education and Practice in Mental Health', *British Journal of Occupational Therapy* 61(9), pp390–2.

Crose PS, 1999, 'Job Characteristics Related to Job Satisfaction in Rehabilitation Nursing', *Rehabilitation Nursing* 24(3), pp95–102.

Dalley J, 1999, 'Evaluation of Clinical Practice – Is a Client-Centred Approach Compatible with Professional Issues?', *Physiotherapy* 85(9), pp491–7.

Davies C, Finlay L & Bullman A (eds), 2000, *Changing Practice in Health and Social Care,* SAGE Publications, London.

Davies J, 2001, 'Waste Not, Want Not', *Health Service Journal* 11 (5757), pp24–7.

Davis CM, 1998, *Patient Practitioner Interaction,* 3rd edn, SLACK Incorporated, New Jersey.

Demerouti E, Bakker AB, Nachreiner F & Schaufeli WB, 2000, 'A Model of Burnout and Life Satisfaction Amongst Nurses', *Journal of Advanced Nursing*, 32(2), pp454–64.

Department of Health, 1989a, *Caring for People: Community Care in the Next Decade and Beyond*, HMSO, London.

Department of Health, 1989b, *Working for Patients, Education and Training, Working Paper 10*, HMSO, London.

Department of Health, 1990, *National Health Service and Community Care Act*, HMSO, London.

Department of Health, 1993, *Targeting Practice: The Contribution of Nurses, Midwives and Health Visitors*, HMSO, London.

Department of Health, 1997a, *The New NHS: Modern, Dependable*, HMSO, London.

Department of Health, 1997b, *Devolution of Responsibilities to Education Consortia*, (Executive Letter) EL(97)30, HMSO, London.

Department of Health, 1998, *A First Class Service: Quality in the NHS*, HMSO, London.

Department of Health, 1999, *The Patients' Charter and You: A Charter for England*, HMSO, London.

Department of Health, 2000a, *A Health Service of all the Talents: Developing the NHS Workforce*, HMSO, London.

Department of Health, 2000b, *Meeting the Challenge: A Strategy for the Allied Health Professions*, HMSO, London.

Department of Health, 2000c, *The NHS Plan – A Plan for Investment, A Plan for Reform*, HMSO, London.

Department of Health, 2000d, *Modernising Regulation – The New Health Professions Council: A Consultation Document*, NHS Executive, Leeds.

Dewar S, 2000, 'Collaborating for Quality: The Need to Strengthen Accountability', *Journal of Interprofessional Care* 14(1), pp31–8.

Dombeck MT, 1997, 'Professional Personhood: Training, Territoriality and Tolerance', *Journal of Interprofessional Care* (11) 1, pp9–21.

Drinka TJK, Miller TF & Goodman BM, 1996, 'Characterizing Motivational Styles of Professionals Who Work on Interdisciplinary Health Care Teams', *Journal of Interprofessional Care* 10(1), pp51–61.

Duffield CM & Lumby J, 1994, 'Context and Culture: The Influence on Role Transition for First Line Managers', *International Journal of Nursing Studies* 31(6), pp555–600.

Dustin D, 2000, 'Managers and Professionals: Another Perspective on Partnership', *Managing Community Care* 8(5), pp14–20.

English National Board for Nursing, Midwifery and Health Visiting (ENB) and Central Council for Education and Training in Social Work (CCETSW), 1992, *A Strategy for Shared Learning*, ENB, London.

Evetts J, 1999, 'Professionalisation and Professionalism: Issues for Interprofessional Care', *Journal of Interprofessional Care* 13(2), pp119–28.

Festinger L, 1957, *A Theory of Cognitive Dissonance*, Harper & Row, New York.

Finlay L, 2000, 'Safe Haven and Battleground: Collaboration and Conflict within the Treatment Team', Davies C, Finlay L & Bullman A (eds), *Changing Practice in Health and Social Care*, SAGE Publications, London.

Fitzpatrick MA, 1996, 'Interdepartmental Collaboration: Focus on Outcomes', *Seminars in Perioperative Nursing* 5(1), pp47–50.

Freidson E, 1994, *Professionalism Reborn: Theory, Prophecy and Policy*, Blackwell, London.

Fulford KWM, Ersser S & Hope T (eds), 1996, *Essential Practice in Patient-Centred Care*, Blackwell Science, Oxford.

Gage M, 1998, 'From Independence to Interdependence: Creating Synergistic Health Care Teams', *Journal of Nursing Administration* 28(4), pp17–26.

General Medical Council (GMC), 2001, *Duties of a Doctor: Guidance from the General Medical Council*, General Medical Council, London.

General Medical Council (GMC), 2001, *Good Medical Practice*, 3rd edn, GMC, London.

Gillam S & Irvine S, 2000, 'Collaboration in the New NHS', *Journal of Interprofessional Care* 14(1), pp5–7.

Glenn S, 2000, 'Partnership and Collaboration in Nursing Education: The Way Forward', Keynote paper, NET Conference.

Gorman P, 1998, *Managing Multi-Disciplinary Teams in the NHS*, Kogan Page, London.

Gough P, 2001, 'Changing Culture and Deprofessionalisation', *Nursing Management* 7(9), pp8–9.

Griffiths R, 1988, *Community Care: Agenda for Action*, HMSO, London.

Grout C, 2000, 'Back-To-Work Basics', *Therapy Weekly*, 27(9), p6.

Hall JA, 1994, 'Factors Related to Job Turnover of Physiotherapists in the West Midlands Region', unpublished MSc Thesis, University of Birmingham.

Hannigan B, 1999, 'Joint Working in Community Mental Health: Prospects and Challenges', *Health and Social Care in the Community* 7(1), pp25–31.

Hart E & Fletcher J, 1999, 'Learning how to change: a selective analysis of literature and experience of how teams learn and organisations change', *Journal of Interprofessional Care* 13(1), pp53–63.

Hawtin S & Moore J, 1998, 'Empowerment or Collusion – the Social Context of Person-Centred Therapy', in Thorne B & Lambers E (eds), *Person-Centred Therapy – A European Perspective*, SAGE Publications, London.

Headrick LA, Knapp M, Neuhauser D, Gelman S, Norman L, Quinn D & Baker R, 1996, 'Working From Upstream to Improve Healthcare: the IHI Interdisciplinary Professional Education Collaborative', *Journal of Quality Improvement* 22(3), pp149–71.

Headrick LA, Wilcock PM, & Batalden PB, 1998, 'Interprofessional Working and Continuing Medical Education', *British Medical Journal* 316, pp771–4.

Health Education Authority, 1997, *Working for Your Health: A Survey of NHS Trust Staff*, HEA, London.

Henneman EA, Lee JL & Cohen JI, 1995, 'Collaboration: A Concept Analysis', *Journal of Advanced Nursing* 21, pp103–9.

Heron J, 1990, *Helping the Client: A Creative Practical Guide*, SAGE Publications, London.

Herzberg F, Mausner B & Snyderman B, 1959, *The Motivation to Work*, 2nd edn, John Wiley & Sons, New York.

Hickling A, 2000, 'Education and Therapy Needs of Children with Multiple Disabilities', *British Journal of Therapy and Rehabilitation* 7(8), pp334–8.

Hilton RW, 1995, 'Fragmentation within Interprofessional Work. A result of Isolationism in Health Care Professional Education Programmes and the Preparation of Students to Function Only in the Confines of their Own Disciplines', *Journal of Interprofessional Care* 9(1), pp33–40.

Horder W, 1996, 'Structures, Cultures and Undertows: Inter-Agency Training for Community Care', *Journal of Interprofessional Care*, 10(2), pp121–32.

Hudson B, 1999, 'Primary Health and Social Care: Working Across Professional Boundaries, Part 1: The Changing Context of Inter-Professional Relationships', *Managing Community Care* 7(1), pp15–22.

Hudson B, 1999, 'Primary Health and Social Care: Working Across Professional Boundaries, Part 2: Models of Inter-Professional Collaboration', *Managing Community Care* 7(2), pp15–20.

Iles V, 1997, *Really Managing Health Care*, Open University Press, Buckingham.

Jack R (ed), 1995, *Empowerment in Community Care*, Chapman Hall, London.

Jennison N, 2001, *Your Career Matters in the NHS: Opportunities in Oxfordshire for Health Care Professionals*, Oxonion Rewley Press, Oxford.

Kamps J, Page R, Seagrove C, Sweet M, Zettergen K & Mackinnon J, 1996, 'Stereotypes Between Physical and Occupational Therapy Students', *Journal of Physical Therapy Education* 10(1), pp18–21.

Kappeli S, 1995, 'Interprofessional Co-operation: Why is Partnership So Difficult?', *Patient Education and Counselling* 26, pp251–6.

Keable D, 1997, *The Management of Anxiety*, 2nd edn, Churchill Livingstone, New York.

Kitchen I & Stancombe R, 1998, 'Dementia Care Mapping in Practice', *Occupational Therapy News*, February, p25.

Kreps GL & Kinimoto EN, 1994, *Effective Communication in Multi-Cultural Health Care Settings*, SAGE Publications, London.

Landau K, 1992, 'Psycho-Physical Strain and the Burnout Phenomenon Amongst Healthcare Professionals', in Estryn-Behar M, Gadbois C & Pottier M (eds), *Ergonomic a l'hopital (Hospital Economics)*, International Symposium, 1991, Editions Octares, Toulouse.

Laungani P & Williams GA, 1997, 'Patient-Focused Care: Effects of Organisational Change on the Stress of Community Health Professionals', *International Journal of Health Education* 35(4), pp108–14.

Law M, Baptiste S & Mills J, 1995, 'Client-Centred Practice: What Does it Mean and Does it Make a Difference?', *Canadian Journal of Occupational Therapy* 62(5), pp250–7.

Leathard A (ed), 1994, *Going Interprofessional: Working Together for Health and Welfare*, Routledge, London.

Lewis RE, Tucker R, Tsao H, Canaan E, Bryant J, Talbot P, King D & Flythe M, 1998, 'Improving the Interdisciplinary Team Process: A Practical Approach to Team Development', *Journal of Allied Health Development*, Spring 1998, pp89–95.

Lichtenstein R, Alexander JA, Jinnett K & Ullmam E, 1997, 'Embedded Intergroup Relations in Interdisciplinary Teams', *Journal of Applied Behavioural Science* 33(4), pp413–34.

Lovelady BM, 1998, 'An Ethnographic Study Exploring the Cultural and Contextual Factors Which Affect Nurses' Decision Making with Respect to Patient Management in the Intensive Care Unit', submitted as part of an

MSc in Advanced Health Care Practice, Oxford Brookes University, Oxford.

Loxley A, 1997, *Collaboration in Health and Welfare: Working with Difference,* Jessica Kingsley Publications, London.

Lurie EE, 1981, 'Nurse Practitioners: Issues in Professional Socialisation', *Journal of Health and Social Behaviour* 22, pp31–48.

Mailick MD & Ashley AA, 1981, 'Politics of Interprofessional Collaboration: Challenge to Advocacy', *Social Casework* 62(3), pp131–7.

Masin ML, 1998, 'Communicating with Cultural Sensitivity', Davis CM, *Patient Practitioner Interaction,* 3rd edn, SLACK Incorporated, New Jersey.

Maslach C, Jackson SE & Leiter MP, 1996, *Maslach Burnout Inventory Manual,* 3rd edn, University of California, Consulting Psychologists Press, Palo Alto.

Maslow AH, 1987, *Motivation and Personality,* 3rd edn, Harper & Row, Cambridge.

McCloskey JC & Maas M, 1998, 'Interdisciplinary Team: The Nursing Perspective is Essential', *Nursing Outlook* 46, pp157–63.

McHugh M, West P, Assatly C, Duprat L, Howard L, Niloff J, Waldo K, Wandel J & Clifford J, 1996, 'Establishing an Interdisciplinary Patient Care Team: Collaboration at the Bedside and Beyond', *Journal of Nursing Administration* 26(4), pp21–7.

McLeod J, 1998, *An introduction to Counselling,* 2nd edn, OU Press, Buckingham.

Meads G & Ashcroft J, 2000, *Relationships in the NHS – Bridging the Gap,* Royal Society of Medicine Press, London.

Melia K, 1987, *Learning and Working: The Occupational Socialisation of Nurses,* Tavistock Publications, London.

Miller A, 2000, 'Multidisciplinary Outcome Measurement: Is It Possible?', *British Journal of Therapy and Rehabilitation* 7(8), pp362–5.

Miller C, Ross N & Freeman M, 1999, 'Shared Learning and Clinical Teamwork: New Directions in Education for Multiprofessional Practice', *Research Reports Series* – No14, English National Board for Nursing, Midwifery and Health Visiting (ENB), London.

Miller C, Ross N & Freeman M, 1999, 'Researching Professional Education: Shared Learning and Clinical Teamwork: New Directions in Education for Multiprofessional Practice', *Research Report Series, No14,* The English National Board for Nursing Midwifery and Health Visiting (ENB), London.

Mills N, Scullion P & Gopee N, 2001, 'Understanding Nursing Roles to Facilitate Collaboration', *British Journal of Therapy and Rehabilitation* 8(1), pp6–11.

Minardi HA & Riley MJ, 1997, *Communication in Health Care: A Skills Based Approach,* Butterworth-Heinemann, Oxford.

Mitchell A, 1995, 'The Therapeutic Relationship in Health Care: Towards a Model of the Process of Treatment', *Journal of Interprofessional Care* 9(1), pp15–20.

Mizrahi T & Abramson S, 1985, 'Sources of Strain Between Physicians and Social Workers: Implications for Social Workers in Health Care Settings', *Social Work in Health Care* 10(3), pp33–51.

National Audit Office, 2001, *Education and Training the Future Health Professions Workforce in England (HC277)*, Stationery Office, London.

Norman IJ & Peck E, 1999, 'Working Together in Adult Community Health Services: An Inter-Professional Dialogue', *Journal of Mental Health* 8(3), pp217–30.

Northcott N, 1999, Organisational Effectiveness – 1, *Nursing Times Learning Curve* 3(2), p10.

Nugent KE & Lambert VA, 1996, 'The Advanced Practice Nurse in Collaborative Practice', *Nursing Connections* 9(1), pp5–15.

Nursing and Midwifery Council, 2002, *Nursing and Midwifery Council Code of Professional Conduct*, NMC, London.

O'Dowd A, 1998, 'Handmaidens and Battleaxes', *Nursing Times* 94(36), pp12–3.

Ogden J, 2001, 'Therapists Hit by Ticking Bomb of Low Pay and High Workload', *Therapy Weekly* 28(2), p1.

Okerlund VW, Jackson PB, Parsons RJ & Corrisa MV, 1995, 'Job Recruitment and Retention Factors for Occupational Therapists in Utah', *American Journal of Occupational Therapy* 49(3), pp263–5.

Onyett S, 1997, 'Collaboration and the Community Mental Health Team', *Journal of Interprofessional Care* 11(3), pp257–67.

Ovretreit J, 1992, *Health Service Quality – An Introduction to Quality Methods for Health Services,* Blackwell Science, Oxford.

Ovretveit J, 1994, 'Pathways to Quality: A Framework for Cost Effective Team Quality Improvement and Multiprofessional Audit', *Journal of Interprofessional Care* 8(3), pp329–33.

Ovretveit J, 1996, 'Five Ways to Describe a Multidisciplinary Team', *Journal of Interprofessional Care* 10 (2), pp163–71.

Ovretveit J, Matthias P & Thompson T (eds), 1997, *Interprofessional Working for Health and Social Care*, Macmillan Press, London.

Owen MJ & Holmes CA, 1993, 'Holism in the Discourse of Nursing', *Journal of Advanced Nursing* 18, pp1688–95.

Oxman AD, 1994, *No Magic Bullets: A Systematic Review of 102 Trials of Inventions to Help Healthcare Professionals Deliver Services More Effectively or Efficiently*, North East Thames Regional Health Authority, London.

Papadopoulos I, Tilki M & Taylor G, 1998, *Transcultural Care A Guide for Health Care Professionals*, Quay Books, Salisbury.

Parton C, 1998, 'Unconditional Positive Regard and its Spiritual Implications', Thorne B & Lambers E (eds), *Person-Centred Therapy – A European Perspective*, SAGE Publications, London.

Patronis Jones R, 1997, 'Multi-Disciplinary Collaboration: Conceptual Development as a Foundation for Patient-Focused Care', *Holistic Nurse Practice* 11(3), pp8–16.

Peck E & Norman IJ, 1999, 'Working Together in Adult Community Mental Health Services: Exploring Inter-Professional Role Relations' *Journal of Mental Health* 8(3), pp231– 42.

Peloquin SM, 1989, 'The Patient-Therapist Relationship in Occupational Therapy: Understanding Visions and Images', *American Journal of Occupational Therapy* 44(1), pp13–21.

Phillips J, 1992, 'Breaking Down the Barriers', *Nursing Times* 88(35), pp30–1.

Phillips P, 1993, 'A Deconstruction of Caring', *Journal of Advanced Nursing* 18, pp1554–8.

Pilgrim D & Waldron L, 1998, 'User Involvement in Mental Health Service Development: How Far Can it Go?', *Journal of Mental Health* 7(1), pp95–104.

Pirrie A, Wilson V, Harden RM & Elsegood J, 1998, 'Multi-Professional Education: Part 2 – Promoting Cohesive Practice in Healthcare' AMEE Guide No12, *Medical Teacher* 20(5), pp 409–16.

Pirrie A, 1999, 'Rocky Mountains and Tired Indians: On Territories and Tribes. Reflections on Multidisciplinary Education in the Health Professions', *British Educational Research Journal* 25(1), pp113–26.

Proctor-Childs T, Freeman M & Miller C, 1998, 'Visions of Teamwork: The Realities of an Interdisciplinary Approach', *British Journal of Therapy and Rehabilitation* 5(12), pp616–8, 635.

Purtilo P & Haddad A, 1996, *Health Professional & Patient Interaction*, 5th edn, WB Saunders Co, Philadelphia.

Reeves S, 2000a, 'Community Based Interprofessional Education for Medical, Nursing and Dental Students', *Health and Social Care in the Community* 8(4), pp269–76.

Reeves S, 2000b, 'A Joint Learning Venture between New Nurses and Junior Doctors', *Nursing Times*, 96(38), pp39–40.

Richardson M, 1999, 'The Symbolism and Myth Surrounding Nurses' Uniform', *British Journal of Nursing* 8(3), pp169–75.

Riley R, 1997, 'Working Together: Inter-Professional Collaboration', *Journal of Child Health Care* 1(4), pp191–4.

Rogers CR, 1980, *A Way of Being,* Houghton Mifflin Company, Boston.

Rokeach M, 1968, *Beliefs, Attitudes and Values,* Jossey-Bass, San Francisco.

Rose M, 2000a, 'Are You Happy in Your Job?', *Therapy Weekly* 27(5), p16.

Rose, M, 2000b, 'Love to Work, Hate the Pay', *Therapy Weekly* 27(6), p12.

Ross F, Rink E & Furne A, 2000, 'Integration or Pragmatic Coalition? An Evaluation of Nursing Teams in Primary Care', *Journal of Interprofessional Care* 14(3), pp257–67.

Rowe H, 1996, 'Multi-Disciplinary Teamwork – Myth or Reality?' *Journal of Nursing Management* 4, pp93–101.

Royal College of Nursing and British Medical Association, 1993, *Cardiopulmonary Resuscitation: A Statement from the RCN and the BMA,* Royal College of Nursing and British Medical Association, London.

Rungadapiachy Dev M, 1999, *Interpersonal Communication and Psychology for Health Care Professionals,* Butterworth-Heinemann, Oxford.

Sabari JS, 1985, 'Professional Socialisation: Implications for Occupational Therapy Education', *American Journal of Occupational Therapy* 39(2), pp96–102.

Saint-Arnaud L, Gingras S, Bailard R, Vezina M & Lee Gosseln H, 1992, 'Les Symptomes Psycholgyues en Milieu Hospitalies' (Psychological Psymptoms in Hospitals), *Ergonomic a l'hopital (Hospital Ergonomics),* International Symposium, Paris 1991, Editions Octares, Toulouse.

Sands RG, Stafford J & McClelland M, 1990, 'I Beg to Differ: Conflict in the Interdisciplinary Team', *Social Work in Health Care* 14(3), pp55–72.

Sealey C, 1999, 'Clinical Governance: An Information Guide for Occupational Therapists', *British Journal of Occupational Therapy* 62(6), pp263–8.

Secord PF & Backman CW, 1964, *Social Psychology,* McGraw-Hill, New York.

REFERENCES

Secretary of State for Health, 1992, *The Health of the Nation*, HMSO, London.

Simmel G, 1904, 'The Sociology of Conflict', *American Journal of Sociology*, 9.

Singleton JK & Green-Hernandez C, 1998, 'Interdisciplinary Education and Practice Has Its Time Come?', *Journal of Nurse-Midwifery* 43(1), pp 3–7.

Spencer, DG and Steers, RM, 1981, 'Performance as a Moderator of the Job Satisfaction-Turnover Relationship', *Journal of Applied Psychology* 66(4), pp511–14.

Standing Committee on Postgraduate Medical and Dental Education (SCOPME), 1997, *Multi-Professional Working and Learning: Sharing the Educational Challenge*, SCOPME, London.

Standing Committee on Postgraduate Medical and Dental Education (SCOPME), 1999, *Equity and Interchange: Multiprofessional Work and Learning*, SCOPME, London.

Stein L, 1967, 'The Doctor-Nurse Game', *Archives of General Psychiatry* 16, pp699–703.

Stewart M, Brown JB, Weston WW, McWhinney IR, McWilliam CL & Freeman TR, 1995, *Patient-Centred Medicine: Transforming the Clinical Method*, SAGE Publications, London.

Sullivan TJ, 1998, *Collaboration: A Health Care Imperative*, McGraw-Hill, London.

Sumsion T, 1999, 'A Study to Determine a British Occupational Therapy Definition of Client-Centred Practice', *British Journal of Occupational Therapy* 62(2), pp52–8.

Sumsion T & Smyth G, 2000, 'Barriers to Client-Centredness and their Resolution', *Canadian Journal of Occupational Therapy* 67(1), pp15–21.

Sundeen SJ, Stuart GW, Ranwin EAD & Cohen SA, 1998, *Nurse-Client Interaction – Implementing the Nursing Process*, 6th edn, Mosby, St Louis.

Swanson JW, 1997, 'Building a Successful Team Through Collaboration', *Nursing Management* 28 (5), pp71–3.

Sweeney K, Stead J & Cosford L, 2000, 'Evidence-Based Practice: Can this Help Joint Working?', *Managing Community Care* 8(5), pp21–7.

Thorne B & Lambers E (eds), 1998, *Person-Centred Therapy – A European Perspective*, SAGE Publications, London.

Tierney AJ & Vallis J, 1999, 'Multidisciplinary Teamworking in the Care of Elderly Patients with Hip Fracture', *Journal of Interprofessional Care* 13(1), pp41–52.

Tuckman BW, 1965, 'Developmental Sequence in Small Groups', *Psychological Bulletin* 63, pp384–99.

United Kingdom Central Council for Nurses, Midwives and Health Visitors (UKCC), 1986, *Project 2000: A Preparation for Practice*, UKCC, London.

United Kingdom Central Council for Nursing, Midwifery and Health Visiting (UKCC), 1992, *The Scope of Professional Practice*, UKCC, London.

United Kingdom Central Council for Nursing, Midwifery and Health Visiting (UKCC), 1996, *Guidelines for Professional Practice*, UKCC, London.

United Kingdom Central Council for Nursing, Midwifery and Health Visiting (UKCC), 2000, *Working Together to Promote Professional Standards*, Register 31 – Spring Issue, UKCC, London.

Walby S, Greenwell J, Mackay L & Soothill K, 1994, *Medicine and Nursing: Professions in a Changing Health Service*, SAGE Publications, London.

Westland, G, 1997, 'Understanding and Surviving Occupational Stress and Burnout', Keable D,*The Management of Anxiety*, 2nd edn, Churchill Livingstone, New York.

Wheeler N & Grice D, 2000, *Management in Health Care*, Stanley Thornes, Cheltenham.

While A & Barriball KL, 1999, 'Qualified and Unqualified Nurses' Views of the Multidisciplinary Team: Findings of a Large Interview Study', *Journal of Interprofessional Care* 13(1), pp77–89.

Whitfield TWA, Allison I, Laing A & Turner PA, 1996, 'Perceptions of the Physiotherapy Profession: A Comparative Study', *Physiotherapy and Practice* 12, pp39–48.

Williams D, 1997, *Communication Skills in Practice: A Practical Guide for Health Professionals*, Jessica Kingsley, London.

Wojner AW, 1996, 'Outcomes Management: An Interdisciplinary Search for Best Practice', *AACN Clinical Issues* 7(1), pp133–45.

Wressle E & Oberg B, 1998, 'Work-Related Stress Among Occupational Therapists in Sweden', *British Journal of Occupational Therapy* 61(10), pp467–72.

Zeldin T, 1999, 'How Work Can be Made Less Frustrating and Conversation Less Boring', *British Medical Journal* 319, pp1633–5.

Zwarenstein M, Atkins J, Barr H, Hammick M, Koppel I & Reeves S, 1999, 'A Systematic Review of Interprofessional Care', *Journal of Interprofessional Care* 13 (4), pp417–24.

Bibliography and Further Reading

Collaborative working

Glen S & Leiba T (eds), *Multi-Professional Learning for Nurses – Breaking the Boundaries,* Palgrave, Hampshire.

Higgs J & Edward H (eds), 1999, *Educating Beginning Practitioners – Challenges for Health Professional Education,* Butterworth-Heinemann.

Mackay L & Webb C, 1995, *Interprofessional Relations in Healthcare,* Edward Arnold, London.

Owens P, Carrier J & Horder J (eds), 1995, *Inter-Professional Issues in Community and Primary Health Care,* Macmillan, London.

Payne M, 2000, *Teamwork in Multi-Professional Care,* Macmillan, London.

Soothill K, Mackay L & Webb C (eds), 1995, *Inter-Professional Relations in Health Care,* Edward Arnold, London.

Aspects of collaborative working

Berglund CA, 1998, *Ethics for Health Care,* OUP, Oxford.

Burnard P, 1995, *Learning Human Skills*, 3rd edn, Butterworth-Heinemann, Oxford.

Burnard P, 1997, *Effective Communication Skills for Health Professionals,* 2nd edn, Chapman Hall, London.

Burns S & Bulman C, 2000, *Reflective Practice in Nursing: The Growth of the Professional Practitioner,* 2nd edn, Blackwell Science, Oxford.

Pettinger R, 2000, *Mastering Organisational Behaviour,* Macmillan, London.

Senge P, 1990, *The Fifth Discipline: The Art and Practice of the Learning Organisation,* Doubleday, New York.
Taylor MC, 2000, *Evidence-Based Practice for Occupational Therapists,* Blackwell Science, Oxford.

Journals: Examples of useful sources
British Educational Research Journal
British Journal of Occupational Therapy
British Journal of Midwifery
British Journal of Nursing
British Journal of Social Work
British Journal of Therapy and Rehabilitation
British Medical Journal
Health and Social Care in the Community
Holistic Nurse Practice
International Journal of Health Education
International Journal of Nursing Studies
Journal of Advanced Nursing
Journal of Applied Psychology
Journal of Health Education
Journal of Interprofessional Care
Managing Community Care
Medical Teacher
Nurse Education Today
Nurse Educator
Nursing Management
Nursing Standard
Nursing Times
Physiotherapy
Physiotherapy Frontline
Practice Nurse
Primary Health Care
Professional Nurse
Quality in Health Care
Therapy Weekly

Websites

Allied Health Professions (CPSM)
http://www.cpsm.org.uk

Allied Health Professions (bulletin)
http://www.doh.gov.uk/ahpbulletin/ahpbulletin01.htm

British Journal of Therapy and Rehabilitation
http://www.bjtr.co.uk

Chartered Society of Physiotherapy (CSP)
http://www.csphysio.org.uk

Cochrane Library and Database of Systematic Reviews
http://www.shef.ac.uk/uni/services/lib/cdfiles/cochrane.html

College of Occupational Therapists
http://www.cot.co.uk

Community Partnerships for Health
http://www.the-network.org

Department of Health
http://www.doh.gov.uk

Department of Health National Service Frameworks (NSFs)
http://www.doh.gov.uk/nsf

Department of Health NHS Modernisation Agency
http://www.modernnhs.nhs.uk

Government Consultation Documents/papers (UK)
http://www.official-publications.co.uk/menu/consult.htm

Health Service Journal
http://www.hsj.co.uk

Journal of Interprofessional Care
http://www.tandf.co.uk.journals
http://www.city.ac.uk/barts/jipc/jipc.htm

King's Fund (what's on and conferences)
http://www.KingsFund.org.uk

NHS National Nursing Leadership Project
http://www.nursingleadership.co.uk

Nursing Times
http://www.nursingtimes.net

Rehabilitation Nursing Journal
http://www.rehabnurse.org

Research development associated with Health Action Zones
http://www.geog.gmw.ac.uk/collabor.html
Social Sciences Information Gateway
http://www.sosig.ac.uk
Therapy Outcomes Collaboration (TOC)
http://members.tripod.co.uk/TOC/members.htm
UK Government Information Services
http://www.open.gov.uk
United Nations
http://www.un.org

Index